Phyllis Driver / Brian McCredie

Besser in Englisch

Profitraining Grammatik

Mit Lösungen

Oberstufe

Cornelsen
SCRIPTOR

Phyllis Driver lebt in München und hat langjährige Erfahrung im Englischunterricht an deutschen Schulen. Sie ist Verfasserin von bewährten Lehrwerken und Übungsprogrammen.

Brian D. McCredie, ehemaliger Verlagsredakteur und Englisch-Dozent, ist Autor zahlreicher Lehrwerke (u. a. über Business-Englisch) sowie eines Sachbuchs über China.

www.cornelsen.de

Bibliografische Information:
Die Deutsche Bibliothek verzeichnet diese Publikation in der Deutschen Nationalbibliografie; detaillierte bibliografische Daten sind im Internet über http://dnb.ddb.de abrufbar.

Dieser Band folgt den Regeln der deutschen Rechtschreibung, die seit August 2006 gelten.

5. 4. 3. 2. 1. Die letzten Ziffern bezeichnen
13 12 11 10 09 Zahl und Jahr der Auflage.

Projektleitung: Stefan Giertzsch, Berlin
Redaktion: Anke Simon, Siegen
Reihengestaltung: tiff.any GmbH, Berlin
Satz und Layout: Ines Schiffel, Berlin
Umschlagentwurf: Patricia Müller, Torsten Lemme, Berlin
Illustrationen: Christine Georg, Dortmund
Druck und Bindearbeiten: orthdruk, Białystok, Polen
Printed in Poland
ISBN 978-3-589-22816-4

Gedruckt auf säurefreiem Papier,
umweltschonend hergestellt aus chlorfrei gebleichten Faserstoffen.

Praktische Tipps zur Arbeit mit diesem Buch
Profitraining Grammatik richtet sich an alle, die größere oder kleinere Probleme mit der englischen Grammatik haben. Können Sie Ihre Meinung zu behandelten Themen nicht richtig äußern, weil Sie sich im Englischen unsicher fühlen? Schneiden Sie bei Klausuren manchmal schlecht ab, weil Sie zu viele sprachliche Fehler machen? Dann wird Ihnen dieses Buch helfen, Ihre englischen Grammatikkenntnisse zu verbessern und zum Profi zu werden.

- ▷ Im **Inhaltsverzeichnis** suchen Sie die Bereiche heraus, die Ihnen besondere Schwierigkeiten im Unterricht bereiten. Die einzelnen Abschnitte können in beliebiger Reihenfolge durchgearbeitet werden.
- ▷ In den Selbstdiagnosetests in **Teil A** (auf den Seiten 6–19) finden Sie alle grammatischen Strukturen, die in diesem Buch angeboten werden. Anhand einer einfachen Übung können Sie herausfinden, ob Sie das grammatische Thema beherrschen. Falls Sie die angegebene Punktzahl nicht erreichen, sollten Sie die Übungen in Teil B sorgfältig durcharbeiten.
- ▷ In **Teil B** (auf den Seiten 20–105) finden Sie Beispielsätze, Erklärungen und Übungen. Hier geht es um Form und Verwendung der jeweiligen grammatischen Strukturen. Die Nummern in den Kreisen bei den Erklärungen beziehen sich auf die vorangegangenen Beispielsätze. Die Übungen in Teil B orientieren sich jeweils an einem bestimmten landeskundlichen Thema. Hier werden viele Wörter wiederholt, die in der Oberstufe vorkommen. So hilft Ihnen *Profitraining Grammatik* auch, Ihre Vokabelkenntnisse aufzufrischen und zu festigen.
- ▷ In **Teil C** (auf den Seiten 106–127) finden Sie zur Wiederholung *Mixed Exercises* (gemischte Übungen), in denen verschiedene grammatische Themen abgefragt werden. Falls Sie dann immer noch Probleme haben, sollten Sie sich die Erklärungen in Teil B nochmals anschauen.
- ▷ Die **Lösungen** (auf den Seiten 128–142) dienen nicht nur der (Selbst-)Kontrolle, sondern sind auch als Hilfe gedacht. Wenn Sie wirklich nicht weiterkommen, können Sie sich die Lösungen anschauen. Das hilft sicherlich eher, als einfach nur zu raten. Bloßes Abschreiben bringt allerdings recht wenig!

Es ist vor allem wichtig, dass Sie die einzelnen Kapitel sorgfältig durcharbeiten. Das geht am besten, wenn man nicht unter Zeitdruck steht, wie es z. B. kurz vor dem Abitur der Fall ist.

Viel Spaß und Erfolg beim Arbeiten mit **Besser in Englisch**!
Die Autoren

1 DIE ZEITEN

Es ist 17 Uhr. James Pond, der berühmte Gentleman und Geheimagent 747, erholt sich gerade beim Fünfuhrtee mit einer Bekannten, als sein Chef ihn anruft.

Bei den unterstrichenen Satzteilen unten handelt es sich um verschiedene Zeitformen der Verben. Streichen Sie jeweils die falsch verwendete Verbform durch.

Boss: James! Thank goodness, I ~~am finding~~/have found[1] you. What on earth are you doing/do you do[2] at Claridge's? ✓

James: I am having/have tea[3] with Mary. It is five o'clock, after all. And you know that I always am having/have[4] tea at five o'clock.

Boss: Well, actually I am trying/have been trying[5] to reach you all day. Have you driven/Were you driving[6] your new car yet?

James: I was going to/will[7] test-drive it at two-thirty, but lunch with Fran lasted/lasts[8] longer than I am expecting/had expected[9] so I didn't drive/hadn't driven[10] it then.

Boss: Thank God! We are believing/believe[11] that Dirty Dick has put/was putting[12] a bomb in it – though we aren't knowing/don't know[13] when or how.

James: Then that explains/has been explaining[14] it! I have seen/saw[15] Dirty Dick this morning at about 10.30. I had taken/have taken[16] the maps from IPW as planned, and have driven/was driving[17] to the garage to pick up my car. Dirty Dick drove/was driving[18] in the other direction when he passed/was passing[19] me. The car hasn't been/wasn't[20] ready when I got there, by the way.

Boss: Well, you aren't going/don't go[21] near it! We are sending/send[22] specialists to look at it in the next couple of hours. Use your old car.

James: But boss, I am driving/have been driving[23] that car for five months! The rear firethrower and the side knives didn't work/don't work/haven't been working[24] properly since August. And the ashtray (= Aschenbecher) has been/is[25] full since July.

Boss: All right. Your new car is going to be/will be[26] ready by eight o'clock this evening.

James: No good. I am going to fly/have flown[27] to Paris this evening. My plane is going to leave/leaves[28] at seven.

Boss: Paris? Aren't you going to/Didn't you[29] photograph the X240 this evening?

James: Don't panic! I will have photographed/will photograph[30] it by then. I am going to do/have done[31] it at 6.15.

Boss: Well, can you phone me from Paris? At around 10.30?

James: At 10.30, boss, I have had/will be having[32] dinner with Jacqueline at Maxim's. It's strictly business, of course. She will have given/is going to give[33] me important information about the XZ774RS this evening. I am going to/will[34] call you at midnight.

Boss: At midnight? No thanks, I am seeing/will see[35] you back here in London. Goodbye.

Your points: /34

▶ Weniger als 34 Punkte? Machen Sie weiter mit Abschnitt 1 **Die Zeiten** in Teil B.

Auch in der Geschichte des Verbrechens findet man, wie überall, so manches Seltsame. Natürlich findet deshalb dieser Bereich auch seinen Platz unter den Weltrekorden.

Bei den unterstrichenen Satzteilen unten handelt es sich um Passivformen. Streichen Sie jeweils die falsch verwendeten Formen durch.

1. The highest bail (= Kaution) which has ever been/~~is ever/would ever be~~ asked for a criminal suspect (= Verdächtige/r) was 46.5 million dollars. ✓
2. This suspect, Antonio de Angeli, accused of/was accused of/would accused of (= anklagen) a huge salad oil swindle.
3. The longest known legal battle (= juristischer Streit) fought/was fought/would fought in Poona, India, from 1205 to 1966.
4. This trial (= Prozess) started because the ancestors (= Vorfahren) of Balasaheb Thorat hadn't been given/hasn't been given/wouldn't have been given the right to preside (= präsidieren) at festivities in his village.
5. The Thorat family is being/be/would be honoured with this right now, as they finally won the battle after over 750 years!
6. $22,000 is estimated/would be estimated/would estimate (= schätzen) to be the highest amount a poacher (= Wilderer) has been fined (= zu einer Geldstrafe verurteilen).
7. This is the amount added up when John Hamburger's car and rifle are confiscated/were confiscated/would confiscated (= beschlagnahmen) by the police.
8. Only two prisoners be/can be/could be kept in the world's smallest prison on the Channel Island of Sark.
9. The only hundredth birthday which has ever been/has ever being/would ever be celebrated in prison was Johnny Weber's in September 1975.
10. Weber had been/is/would imprisoned in 1926 and had spent fifty-one years in prison by his 100th birthday.
11. The greatest forgery (= Fälschung) which has ever been/is ever been/would recorded was during World War II.
12. £150,000,000 worth of £5 notes been/were/would be printed by Nazi forgers under the code name 'Bernhard'.
13. Who knows how much money is/will be/would forged in the years to come?
14. The greatest robbery on record carried out/was carried out/would be carried out in June 1945.
15. At this time almost $10,000,000 was being taken/was taken/would be taken from the Reichsbank by a mixed American-German group of thieves.

Your points: ______ /14

▶ Weniger als 14 Punkte? Dann machen Sie weiter mit Abschnitt 2 **Das Passiv** in Teil B.

3 DIE INDIREKTE REDE

Ursula, eine Studentin an der Universität, hat als Bestandteil einer Studie über das Kriminalwesen einige New Yorker Polizisten interviewt. In diesem Bericht gibt sie die Aussagen von zwei Polizisten wieder.

Bei den unterstrichenen Satzteilen unten handelt es sich um Zeitformen in der indirekten Rede. Streichen Sie jeweils die falsch verwendeten Formen durch.

Victor McGillis, policeman*:* "As a child I dreamed of becoming a policeman. And when I started ten years ago, I just wasn't the type to do anything else. Even now, I still think it's one of the most gratifying jobs in the world. I've been accused of being a hypocrite. But I'm just a human being with a job."

Ursula: Victor McGillis said that as a child he/~~I~~[1] had dreamed/was dreaming[2] of becoming a policeman. He also asked/stated[3] that he hadn't been/wasn't[4] the type to do anything else. He claimed it had been/is/was[5] one of the most gratifying jobs in the world. He told/told me[6] he had been/has been/was[7] accused of being a hypocrite, but he felt he had been/has been/was[8] just a human being with a job. ✓

Charles Washington, ex-policeman: "About seven years ago, I became a police officer because of the opportunity it gave a young African American who didn't have a college education. It was very easy for me to find dice games (= Würfelspiel), prostitutes or narcotics (= Droge) in the community because any African American can find them. But I soon learned that white Americans control the crime here, and they make most of the money. Take the Churchill case several years ago. We arrested four African Americans who had been involved in a drug deal. But the real people responsible were white – Ciardi and Cleighton. They're living free, rich and happy now somewhere in South America. That's when I decided to quit."

Ursula: Charles Washington said he became/had become/was becoming[9] a policeman because of the opportunity it did give/had given/gave[10] him as a young African American. He said it had been/has been[11] very easy then for him to find crime in the community because any African American could/did[12]. But he stated that he had learned/has learned[13] that white Americans were in control of crime. Charles reported that they/we[14] arrested/had arrested[15] four African Americans who had/have[16] been involved in a drug deal some years ago. But he felt sure that the whites who had/have[17] been responsible are/were[18] living free, rich and happy in South America.

Your points: ______ /17

▶ Weniger als 17 Punkte? Dann machen Sie weiter mit Abschnitt 3 **Die indirekte Rede** in Teil B.

Märchen und Sagen enthalten fast immer ein Element des Bösen. Man will damit lehren, dass Ungehorsam und Leichtsinn manches Unheil zur Folge haben können. Viele dieser Geschichten wären besser ausgegangen, wenn die Warnungen befolgt worden wären und die Hauptpersonen vernünftiger gehandelt hätten.

Bei den folgenden Sätzen handelt es sich um *if*-Sätze. Streichen Sie jeweils von den unterstrichenen Formen die falsch verwendeten durch.

1. Hansel und Gretel, if you go/~~went/will go~~ too far into the dark forest, something terrible happened/happens/will happen. ✓
2. If you build/built/will build your house out of sticks or straw (= Stroh), little pigs, the wolf blew/blows/will blow it down.
3. Cinderella, if you stay/will stay/would stay at the ball after midnight, people are seeing/see/will see that you are only a poor girl in rags (= Lumpen).
4. Something terrible happened/happens/will happen if Pandora opened/opens/will open that box.
5. You have learned/learned/might learn something painful if you look/looked/would look too long for the truth, Oedipus.
6. What did/will/would you do if a wolf in a dark forest asked/will ask/would ask you where you were going?
7. If my stepmother (= Stiefmutter) asked/asks/would ask me to do all the housework, I am moving/moved/would move out!
8. If a strange, old woman might offer/offered/would offer me a big, red apple, I certainly didn't take/won't take/wouldn't take it.
9. If my father tells/told/would tell a king that I could spin straw into gold, I am telling/told/would tell the king my father was crazy.
10. I ran/will run/would run away if someone told/will tell/would tell me to live with a beast.
11. If the prince didn't kiss/hadn't kissed/wouldn't kiss Sleeping Beauty (= Dornröschen), she slept/will sleep/would have slept forever.
12. The people of Hamelin hadn't lost/wouldn't lose/wouldn't have lost their children if they had kept/would keep/would have kept their promise.
13. If Cinderella hadn't lost/wouldn't lose/wouldn't have lost her shoe, the prince hadn't found/wouldn't find/wouldn't have found her.
14. The princess hadn't found/won't find/wouldn't have found her handsome prince if she didn't kiss/hadn't kissed/wouldn't have kissed a frog.

Your points: ______ /27

▶ Weniger als 27 Punkte? Dann machen Sie weiter mit Abschnitt **4 *If*-Sätze** in Teil B.

Einige der spannendsten Geschichten überhaupt handeln von den ungelösten Geheimnissen dieser Welt. Hier findet man Berichte über Leute, die von selbst in Flammen aufgingen und verbrannten, und Augenzeugenberichte darüber, wie es Fische vom Himmel regnete.

Bei den unterstrichenen Satzteilen unten handelt es sich um modale Hilfsverben. Streichen Sie jeweils die falsch verwendeten modalen Hilfsverbformen durch.

There are many phenomena in the world that scientists have never ~~able to~~/been able to/~~could~~[1] explain fully. The human body can/is said/man says[2] not to burn completely under 1,560 °C, a very extreme heat. Yet there are cases of bodies which have burned up completely by themselves while surrounding objects, which have ought to/ought have/ought to have[3] burned as well, were left unharmed. Some people can/can be able to/will can[4] walk through fire although according to laws of science they shall/had better/are supposed to[5] burn. ✓

We all know that you have/must/shall[6] to connect an electric light to a source of electricity to turn it on. Brian Williams of Cardiff, however, made headlines in 1952 when he was able to/could[7] light a light bulb (= Glühbirne) just by holding it in his hands. Perhaps you could/had/would[8] better not shake/to shake[9] his hand while standing in the rain!

The famous Voynich Manuscript may be/have been/was[10] written by the mysterious Franciscan monk Roger Bacon in the thirteenth century. Even after years of work the best scientists have could not/been not able/not been able to[11] decipher (= entziffern) its code. Many people think that alchemists were used to/did before/used to[12] perform secret rites with this mysterious work.

If you are used to walk/to walking/walking[13] in the rain without an umbrella, you better/had better/had better to[14] be careful. There are saying/are supposed to/should[15] be people who have experienced fish raining from the sky. Scientists think this must been/have been/to have been[16] caused by tornados sucking (= saugen) the fish up from the sea.

Would you can/could/be able to[17] tell the future from Tarot cards, stars, stones or tea leaves? Some people are use to/are used to/used to[18] looking at these signs before making any decision. It is/can/shall be[19] said that even today some people practise black magic to take revenge on their enemies. You ought/shall/should[20] stay away from such people. If you know someone who might practise black magic, you don't have/mustn't/needn't[21] let/to let[22] them have your hair or fingernails! And if you want to practise black magic, you will have/must/need[23] keep it a secret. Witches are no more popular today than they used to be/were used to being[24] in the Middle Ages. Shall/Will[25] I tell you more, or are you too frightened? You needn't to/needn't/mustn't to[26] worry. This is the end of the exercise.

Your points: /25

▶ Weniger als 25 Punkte? Dann machen Sie weiter mit Abschnitt 5 **Modale Hilfsverben** in Teil B.

1922 entdeckten die britischen Archäologen (= archeologist) Howard Carter und Lord Carnarvon das prachtvolle Pharaonengrab des vor dreitausend Jahren gestorbenen Tut-ench-Amun im Tal der Könige (= Valley of the Kings) in Ägypten. Sie haben Gegenstände von großem Wert aus dem Grab (= tomb) genommen und verkauft und dabei – wie heute noch behauptet wird – den Todesfluch des Pharaos heraufbeschworen!

Bei den unterstrichenen Satzteilen unten handelt es sich jeweils um verschiedene Entsprechungen für „lassen“ (zulassen; machen lassen; veranlassen, dass etwas getan wird). Korrigieren Sie alle Fehler. (Achten Sie auch auf die Wortstellung!)

The Egyptian Government let the two Englishmen excavate[1] (= ausgraben) in the Valley of the Kings in the south of the country. ✓ They allowed them to start[2] work in 1917 and permitted them ✓ search for[3] the tomb of Tutankhamen. Carter had an area marking out[4] and had that excavate[5] inch by inch. During the next five years he got tons of rock removed[6] by his Egyptian workmen. In late 1922 Carter discovered a step cut in the ground – he had his workers uncover[7] (= freilegen) several more steps and made them to clear away[8] as many rocks as possible. On November 5th, 1922, the door to the tomb was found.
The archeologists allowed only a few outsiders being[9] present when, finally, they had opened[10] the door by their workmen. Inside was a treasure worth millions. Those who were present said it almost made cry[11] Carter to see it. Carter and Carnarvon got most of it transported[12] to Cairo, but they didn't permit the Egyptians keeping[13] everything. In fact, they kept some very valuable pieces for themselves. Carter later got an American museum to pay[14] a large amount for some of these pieces.
Several people close to Carter and Carnarvon died very suddenly and unexpectedly after the tomb was opened. The newspapers said Tutankhamen them had had killed[15]. It was the curse of the Pharaohs! Lord Carnarvon died in April, 1923 (at the moment of his death something happened – nobody could ever explain it – which made all lights in Cairo going out[16]!). Then Carnarvon's half-brother died, followed by Carnarvon's wife, a close friend of Carter's, and finally Carter himself, who became ill and never recovered.

Your points: /14

▶ Weniger als 14 Punkte? Dann machen Sie weiter mit Abschnitt 6 **Das Verb „lassen“** in Teil B.

7 DAS GERUNDIUM UND DER INFINITIV

Seit seinem Tod im Jahre 1957 ist Humphrey Bogart zu einer Kultfigur des amerikanischen Films geworden. Berühmt wurde er durch zahlreiche Rollen in den 1940er und frühen 1950er Jahren, vor allem als zynischer Gangster bzw. als zäher Privatdetektiv.

Bei den unterstrichenen Satzteilen unten handelt es sich um den Infinitiv, das Gerundium und um bestimmte Präpositionen, die immer in Verbindung mit einem Gerundium stehen. Streichen Sie alle falschen Lösungen durch. Es gilt jeweils nur eine Lösung.

There's no ~~deny~~/denying[1] that Humphrey Bogart ('Bogie') was and is the perfect hero for a dis- ✓
illusioned era. He was keen ~~in~~/on/~~to~~[2] acting from the very start – by the time he was one year ✓
old he was already used with/to/of[3] appearing in advertisements for baby food! His father, an eminent New York doctor, was a man who believed in/of/at[4] working hard and hoped his son would concentrate with/from/on[5] getting to Yale University.
But Bogart usually never felt like to do/doing[6] what others expected him to do/doing[7], so he decided to become/becoming[8] an actor instead. After several years on Broadway, where he failed (= es nicht schaffen) to make/making[9] much of an impression, he went to Hollywood in 1929 and there kept to play/playing[10] unimportant roles (mainly as a gangster, once as a vampire!) till someone suggested to give/giving[11] him the starring role in *High Sierra* (1941). For years the film studios had felt it wasn't worth to offer/offering[12] Bogart an important part as there was no possibility of/with/to[13] his succeeding at it. But *High Sierra*, which is now considered to be/being[14] one of his best films, was a great success and he was soon busy to shoot/shooting[15] (= drehen) those films that made him the world's most famous tough guy, such as *Casablanca* (1943) and *The Big Sleep* (1946). Although Bogart would probably hate to admit/admitting[16] it if he was alive today, he was – in private – not at all tough and he resented (= übel nehmen) people to see/seeing[17] him in that light. It's true that he could never resist (= widerstehen) to tell/telling[18] people he disliked what he thought of them. Most of us, of course, would prefer not to annoy/annoying[19] the boss, but Bogart was a rebel and just couldn't help (= nicht umhinkönnen) to open/opening[20] his mouth if he didn't like someone. Nobody could stop him for/at/from[21] doing what he wanted – it was all part of the tough-guy image.

Your points: ______ /19

▶ Weniger als 19 Punkte? Dann machen Sie weiter mit Abschnitt 7 **Das Gerundium und der Infinitiv** in Teil B.

Scotland Yard, das Hauptquartier der Londoner Polizei, existiert seit 1829. Seit seiner Gründung hat Scotland Yard eine Vorreiterrolle in der Anwendung von modernen Methoden der Verbrechensbekämpfung gespielt.

Bei den unterstrichenen Satzteilen unten handelt es sich um Adverbial- bzw. Relativsätze. In Klammern steht dafür jeweils eine Partizipialverkürzung. Streichen Sie die Verkürzungen in den Sätzen durch, in denen nur die lange Form richtig ist.

Sir Robert Peel created the London police in 1829. Because he realized (Realizing) [1] the urgent need for this, he established a force of 1000 'bobbies'. But only those people who were living (living) [2] in Central London were actually the responsibility of the bobbies. The number of policemen grew quickly. Before they were able to (being able to) [3] reduce London's crime, they had to win the confidence (= Vertrauen) of the Londoners. Although they found (Although finding) [4] this difficult at first, they succeeded and were soon responsible for law and order among two and a half million people. The bobbies, in their blue uniforms and tall hats, became a familiar (=vertraut) sight. After they had arrived (After arriving) [5] on the scene in 1829, they managed to catch some of the capital's worst criminals. The number of crimes that were solved (solved) [6] in London increased dramatically. Most of those who had been arrested (been arrested) [7] once never caused trouble again in London's streets. Scotland Yard's police officers started to win respect all over the world.
If they were given (If given) [8] a difficult case, it was not often that they were unsuccessful. Although they didn't manage (Although not managed) [9] to get Jack the Ripper – the killer who was hunted (hunted) [10] by the police for the brutal murder of at least five women in 1888 – they did get lots of other criminals.
The use of fingerprints (= Fingerabdruck) to catch criminals is one of the scientific methods which was introduced (introduced) [11] by Scotland Yard in 1901, and which was copied (copied) [12] by police forces all over the world. Scotland Yard first presented the so-called Galton-Henry fingerprint system publicly in 1900, and they hoped (hoping) [13] it would revolutionize police methods. And it did! Scotland Yard moved to a new building in 1890. As it had grown (Having grown) [14] even bigger by the 1960s, it moved once again in 1967, to its present location near Victoria Street in Central London.

✓

Your points: ______ /13

▶ Weniger als 13 Punkte? Dann machen Sie weiter mit Abschnitt 8 **Das Partizip** in Teil B.

9 RELATIVSÄTZE

Edgar Allan Poe wird als einer der ersten modernen Schriftsteller überhaupt betrachtet – modern deshalb, weil er in Form von oft grauenerregenden Geschichten die menschliche Psyche untersucht.

Streichen Sie in diesem Text jedes falsch verwendete Relativpronomen durch. Es gilt jeweils nur eine Lösung.

Edgar Allan Poe, ~~that~~/who [1] was born in Boston in 1809 and which/who [2] died mysteriously at the age of 40 in Richmond, Virginia, is an author whose/that [3] is now recognized as being one of the greatest who/which [4] ever lived. ✓
Poe, who/whom [5] loved to play practical jokes, usually dressed in the very unamusing colour black, what/which [6] made his sad face look even sadder (at least according to those few people which/who [7] have left a description of him). It was this rather bizarre person who/whose [8] works (which/who [9] were not fully understood until after his death) influenced the great French poet, Baudelaire, as well as Sir Arthur Conan Doyle, both of who/whom/which [10] admired Poe. Conan Doyle, which/whose [11] figure of Sherlock Holmes is perhaps the world's most famous private detective, found a model on that/whose/which [12] to base his hero in Poe's Auguste Dupin, who/that [13] is in every way as brilliant as Holmes.
Of the short stories in whom/which [14] the French detective appears, *The Murders in the Rue Morgue* is the one who/which [15] is known best. In this short story, that/who/which [16] was published in 1841 and with whom/whose [17] hero, Dupin, Sherlock Holmes can certainly be identified, Poe created one of the first modern crime stories. The brilliant Dupin quickly solves the mystery of the two women that/which/whom [18] have been brutally killed in the Rue Morgue by ... an orangutan, what/that/which [19] must be one of the strangest murders in literature!

Your points: /18

▶ Weniger als 18 Punkte? Dann machen Sie weiter mit Abschnitt 9 **Relativsätze** in Teil B.

Die sogenannte Prohibition in den USA dauerte von 1920 bis 1933. Während dieser Zeit war jeglicher Verkauf von alkoholischen Getränken strengstens verboten. Das neue Gesetz führte aber dazu, dass die Kriminalitätsrate in diesen Jahren rapide anstieg.

An den unterstrichenen Stellen im folgenden Text muss ein Adverb oder ein Adjektiv stehen. Aber Vorsicht – manchmal müssen Sie zwischen zwei Adverbien (mit zwei Formen und zwei verschiedenen Bedeutungen) wählen.

'Prohibition' in the USA was the result of a law that forbade the sale of alcohol, but it was a law that can ~~hard~~/hardly[1] be called a success. Until January 1920, alcohol had been free/freely[2] ✓ available to adults in the USA. But when direct/directly[3] Prohibition began, it became impossible/impossibly[4] to obtain alcohol legally. In fact, the new law opened the gates wide/widely[5] for the so-called 'bootleggers' (= Alkoholschmuggler, AE). It soon seemed clear/clearly[6] that certain US cities – especially Chicago – were moving close/closely[7] to a situation where gangsters were taking control of near/nearly[8] everything. In spite of all the efforts to prevent the sale of illegal alcohol, it never ran short/shortly[9]. In 1929 the Depression began, crime increased and things looked hopeless/hopelessly[10] for the forces of law and order. It had actually become dangerous/dangerously[11] to walk along some of Chicago's best-known streets in daylight, which may sound unbelievable/unbelievably[12] but is nevertheless a fact. Crime in Chicago was in the hands of Al Capone, who was pretty/prettily[13] brutal (even by today's standards). In the St Valentine's Day Massacre of February 14th, 1929, for example, he had seven men shot in cold blood – just/justly[14] like that! Capone most/mostly[15] made his money by bootlegging, prostitution, and gambling. In 1934 he was sent to Alcatraz Federal Prison for tax evasion (= Steuerhinterziehung). He died in Miami in 1947.

Your points: /14

▶ Weniger als 14 Punkte? Dann machen Sie weiter mit Abschnitt 10 **Adverbien** in Teil B.

In der zweiten Hälfte des 19. Jahrhunderts ergoss sich ein schier unaufhaltsamer Strom von weißen Siedlern in den „Wilden Westen“ der USA. Mit den Siedlern kamen Revolverhelden (= gunman) und Bankräuber, aber auch die legendär gewordenen Gesetzeshüter wie Wyatt Earp (1848–1929).

Im folgenden Text müssen Sie entscheiden, welches Adverb zu dem vorangehenden Verb gehört. Streichen Sie alle falschen Lösungen durch.

Nowadays historians are quick to point ~~off~~/out/~~over~~ [1] that most people who went to the 'Wild West' between 1850 and 1900 did so in order to settle away/off/down [2] there, as well as to bring up/down/back [3] their children in a region with great economic potential. There were relatively few criminals among them. But some, like the brothers Frank and Jesse James, were real killers, who managed to get with/over/away [4] after every robbery and seemed to turn through/down/up [5] just when the law expected them least. Between 1866 and 1872 they robbed eight banks. Jesse, who was murdered in 1882, soon built round/up/off [6] a reputation as a sort of Robin Hood.
One of the West's most famous marshalls was Wyatt Earp. He was a quiet, modest (= bescheiden) man, who never found it necessary to show away/up/off [7] and who succeeded in cleaning down/up/ahead [8] such notorious (= berüchtigt) places as Dodge City (Kansas) and Tombstone (Arizona). Cowboys who came to town for a drink had to check in/away/through [9] their guns at the marshall's office, and these were only given in/back/off [10] to them when they left. Saloons that disregarded (= nicht beachten) the law about guns were closed in/out/down [11] for a few days.
Earp, himself a former gunman, was anything but a model citizen – in Dodge City, for example, he set back/down/up [12] his own brothel (= Bordell)! But Earp and his brothers were fearless and would never give ahead/in/through [13] if they were faced with a dangerous situation. The Earps became an American legend when, in a sixty-second long gun battle at the OK Corral on October 26th, 1881, they carried round/in/out [14] their promise to destroy a gang of notorious gunmen. Earp died quietly, at home in bed, in 1929.

Your points: /13

▶ Weniger als 13 Punkte? Dann machen Sie weiter mit Abschnitt 11 ***Phrasal verbs*** in Teil B.

Meist werden Ritter als Helden dargestellt. G. K. Chesterton aber hat eine Geschichte von einem geächteten Ritter erzählt, dessen Stärke es war, schnell aufzutauchen, um dann genauso schnell wieder zu verschwinden. Erst als ein Drache die Stadt bedrohte, lernte die Bevölkerung diese eher lästige Eigenschaft zu schätzen.

Setzen Sie im folgenden Text jeweils the ein, wo es notwendig ist.

The [1] **Dragon and** _____ [2] **outlaw** (= geächtet) **Knight** ✓

Once upon a time, there was a famous knight who was an outlaw, and very good at _____ [3] hiding. _____ [4] L/life of this knight was so wild and lawless that he had difficulty getting to _____ [5] church punctually on _____ [6] Sunday. And _____ [7] way he arrived in _____ [8] church was quite unusual anyway. He would come crashing in through _____ [9] stained-glass windows, or drop suddenly out of _____ [10] belfry (= Glockenturm) where he had been hiding, almost on to _____ [11] heads of _____ [12] worshippers (= Kirchgänger). It always frightened _____ [13] old lady playing _____ [14] organ. But _____ [15] most people said that even _____ [16] criminals must get to _____ [17] church somehow. _____ [18] K/knight became better and better at _____ [19] appearing and disappearing, even at _____ [20] elections (= Wahl) and _____ [21] coronations (= Krönung). _____ [22] P/police were never able to find _____ [23] holes where he hid himself, and were quite desperate. But, of course, nobody wanted to arrest him in _____ [24] church, the only place they would have had time to do so. Well, one day, _____ [25] most terrible thing in _____ [26] history of this region happened – a dragon appeared. He trampled _____ [27] walls and castles, destroyed _____ [28] beautiful things and killed _____ [29] people. When he finally came near _____ [30] capital, _____ [31] king and his nobles (= Edelmann) climbed up _____ [32] towers and trees closest to them, a very silly thing to do, as this dragon had a reputation (= Ruf) for knocking down _____ [33] towers and trees in a minute. In _____ [34] end, who do you think saved _____ [35] population from _____ [36] dragon? Nobody except _____ [37] kings's daughter saw it, because all of _____ [38] other people were hiding. But they were all surprised when _____ [39] terrible dragon started to act tame suddenly, and ended up in, of all places, _____ [40] church. After breaking a few of _____ [41] windows, by accident probably, he knelt quite peacably at ______ [42] altar. And when nobody could find ______ [43] criminal knight, they believed ______ [44] story of ______ [45] princess. She said that ______ [46] knight who could get in and out everywhere, had found his way into ______ [47] most unusual hiding place of all. And this clever knight had tamed the dragon, from ______ [48] inside, of course.

Your points: ______ /47

▶ Weniger als 47 Punkte? Dann machen Sie weiter mit Abschnitt 12 **Der bestimmte Artikel** in Teil B.

13 MENGENANGABEN

Seit uralten Zeiten symbolisiert der Drache meist das Böse. Man dachte an Fabelwesen, Ungeheuer oder überlebende Bestien aus prähistorischer Zeit. Und so wurde der Drache beschrieben, sowohl im Märchen als auch in wissenschaftlichen Arbeiten.

Bei den unterstrichenen Satzteilen unten handelt es sich um unbestimmte Mengenangaben. Streichen Sie jeweils die falsch verwendeten Wörter durch. Es gibt jeweils nur eine Lösung.

Until about three hundred years ago, a lot of/~~much~~ [1] people believed that dragons existed. ✓ Many/Much [2] of what they believed about dragons came from many/much [3] different stories of strange beasts seen on foreign travels. All/Each [4] story may have started with any/some [5] truth, but with all/each [6] time it was told it became more/most [7] exaggerated. In addition, people knew not anything/nothing [8] about dinosaurs, and there wasn't any/some [9] other explanation for the huge bones that were occasionally found.
Most/Much [10] Greeks and Romans had very few/less/little [11] doubt that dragons existed. The Roman writer Pliny collected any/some [12] stories about dragons in his *Natural History* around 70 AD. Any/A few [13] of these concerned huge dragons in India who would attack and kill any/some [14] elephant they met. In ancient Greek legend, Jason had to sow a field with any/some [15] dragons' teeth, and when he finished, any/every [16] tooth turned into a soldier. Strangely, although dragons were even more/most [17] important in Chinese traditions, there were less/fewer [18] stories about them. In China, it was believed that all/everything [19] related to clouds, rain and lightning came from dragon breath.
In Danish legend, the fewest/least [20] bit of poison (= Gift) from the dragon Fafnis' mouth would kill any/some [21] man instantly. In a Brothers Grimm tale, three soldiers who had deserted because of very few/less/little [22] pay (= Lohn), were rescued by a dragon who showed them how to get as many/much [23] money as they wanted. Every/Some [24] dragons transformed back and forth into beautiful ladies. This was a problem for L. P. Hartley's hero, Conrad, who hadn't any/some [25] idea that the ugly dragon he killed was actually the beautiful woman he had loved.
In the sixties, many/more [26] people enjoyed the folksong about Puff, the Magic Dragon. Puff was certainly fewer/least/less [27] dangerous than more/most [28] dragons you read of in fairy tales. Needless to say, there aren't many/much [29] stories about dragons told these days.

Your points: ______ /28

▶ Weniger als 28 Punkte? Dann machen Sie weiter mit Abschnitt 13 **Mengenangaben** in Teil B.

1 DIE ZEITEN

Thema: Celebrations

1.1 Das *simple present* und das *present progressive*

Read the examples

1. Most people **love** a celebration.
2. This year, Easter **falls** on the 15th of April.
3. My father **doesn't** usually **celebrate** his birthday.
4. **Does** our plane **leave** at 3 p.m. or at 4 p.m.?
5. Don't bother your mother! She's **making** Christmas cookies.
6. **Are** you **spending** Christmas at home this year?
7. Our neighbours **have** a pink Xmas tree this year. It's awful!

Remember

Das ***simple present*** wird verwendet für:

- ▷ feststehende Tatsachen, Zustände oder Gesetzmäßigkeiten ❶ ❷,
- ▷ gewohnheitsmäßige oder regelmäßige Geschehnisse ❸,
- ▷ künftiges Geschehen, wenn dieses durch einen Zeitplan, z. B. Fahrplan oder Stundenplan, festgelegt ist ❹.

Das ***present progressive*** wird verwendet für:

- ▷ einen Vorgang, der im Moment des Sprechens oder Schreibens abläuft oder von begrenzter Dauer ist ❺,
- ▷ eine einmalige zukünftige Handlung, in Verbindung mit einer Zeitangabe ❻.

Verben, die keine Handlung, sondern einen **Zustand** ausdrücken, wie be, love, like, know, hate, have (im Sinne von „besitzen"), werden in der Regel nicht in der *progressive form* benutzt ❶ ❷ ❼.
Die Verben live and work können dagegen auf permanente und gleichzeitig aktuelle Situationen deuten, und beide Formen sind meistens passend.

1 **Es folgen Ausschnitte aus Gesprächen über Weihnachtsfeiern in verschiedenen Ländern. Setzen Sie die richtigen Verbformen ein.**

1. In Italy, people *eat* (eat) and ______ (drink) very little the day before Christmas.
2. But Mrs Lepori ______ (prepare) many special fish dishes for a lot of guests this year.

3. A witch, *La Befana*, ______ (fly) down the chimney (= Kamin) and ______ (give) the children presents on 6th January.
4. – ______ (the Leporis/make) presents for the children every Christmas?
   – They usually ______ (do), but this year they haven't got time, so they ______ (buy) them.
5. In Spain families ______ (eat) a big meal after midnight on Christmas Eve.
6. It's only 20th December, but Mercedes del Rio ______ (cook) special dishes for this feast. It's hard work, but she ______ (like) it!
7. Her husband Juan ______ (dress) as a wise man (= einer der Heiligen Drei Könige) this year to bring the children their presents on 6th January.
8. It's a new experience for him. Usually his brother Carlos ______ (do) this pleasant job.
9. – In France, ______ (children/receive) their presents on 25th December, like in the USA? – No, they ______ (not do). They ______ (receive) their presents on St Nicholas' Day, 6th December.
10. The Du Pont family are French, but they ______ (live) in Detroit now, so this year the children ______ (celebrate) Christmas like American children.
11. This year the Du Ponts ______ (not keep) their tradition of *le reveillon*, the meal after the Christmas Eve midnight mass (= Gottesdienst).
12. In Australia it is so hot on Christmas Day that families usually ______ (eat) lunch on the beach. We ______ (know) the perfect beach for it.
13. – ______ (they/have) a Christmas tree? – No, they ______ (not do). But they ______ (decorate) the house with seasonal Australian plants called Christmas bush and Christmas bell.
14. This year Mr and Mrs McCarthy ______ (go) with the whole family to Bali for a change. Their tour ______ (start) on 23rd December and ______ (finish) on 6th January.
15. ______ (children/look forward to) it?

16. In Mexico, Christmas celebrations ______ (start) on 16th December by remembering Mary and Joseph's search for an inn.

17. – Maria Sanchez is very busy now. She ______ (make) a *pinata*. – I ______ (not understand). What ______ (she/make)? – A *pinata*. These are decorated containers full of little presents for the children, which they always ______ (break) open blindfolded (= mit verbundenen Augen) at their Christmas parties.

1.2 Das *simple past* und das *past progressive*

Read the examples

1. I **travelled** by train to Cranesville last Christmas.
2. What **was** she **doing** at 10 o'clock last night? She **was reading**!
3. The guitarist **was playing** his solo when the sound system **broke** down.
4. They **were sitting** in the park, the **sun was shining**, and the children **were playing**. Suddenly they heard a scream.

Remember

Das ***simple past*** wird verwendet, um zu berichten, dass etwas zu einer bestimmten Zeit in der Vergangenheit passierte ❶.

Das ***past progressive*** beschreibt, was zu einer bestimmten Zeit in der Vergangenheit für einige Zeit vor sich ging ❷ oder was schon im Gange war, als etwas anderes geschah. Der zweite Vorgang steht im ***simple past*** ❸.

Das ***past progressive*** wird auch für mehrere gleichzeitig ablaufende Vorgänge gebraucht. Das ist oft für Hintergrundgeschehen in Erzählungen oder Berichten der Fall ❹.

2 In den USA sieht man in der Vorweihnachtszeit besonders in den Einkaufszentren viele als Weihnachtsmänner verkleidete Personen. Sie läuten Glocken und sammeln für die Caritas. Diese Verkleidung nutzen natürlich auch einige Diebe, um auf diese Weise maskiert ihrem Gewerbe nachzugehen. So ist es auch in dieser kleinen Geschichte über einen Banküberfall in einer Kleinstadt, die wir Cranesville nennen wollen.

Setzen Sie die richtigen Verbformen ein.

It *was* 1 (be) three days before Christmas, and in the small town of Cranesville everybody *was getting* 2 (get) ready for the holidays. Mothers ______ 3 (bake) Christmas goodies, and fathers ______ 4 (put) together model trains. Kids ______ 5 (practise) for school Christmas plays and ______ 6 (try) to stay on their best behaviour. Men in Santa Claus suits ______ 7 (stand) on street corners, ______ 8 (ring) bells and ______ 9 (ask) for donations (= Spende) to charities (= Wohltätigkeitsverein). Bank employees ______ 10 (give) out more money than usual to last-minute shoppers.
And that's just how the caper (= Ding, Gaunerei) ______ 11 (happen).
At 9 a.m. there ______ 12 (be) only about two or three shoppers passing to give money to the Santa Claus who ______ 13 (stand) near the First National Bank on Ott Street. Inside the bank, Oliver Buswell ______ 14 (count) his money in the till (= Kasse), when a man in a Santa Claus suit ______ 15 (come) in.
"Merry Christmas," ______ 16 (say) Oliver, and then he ______ 17 (see) that the man ______ 18 (point) a gun at him. Santa ______ 19 (ask) him to hand over all his money. Oliver ______ 20 (look) at his two colleagues, but Alice ______ 21 (count) money and ______ 22 (not notice) him, and Arthur ______ 23 (get) a cup of coffee from the machine. There ______ 24 (not be) any other customers in the bank. Santa ______ 25 (get) more and more impatient. So poor Oliver ______ 26 (hand) over $15,000 – a nice present! Later that day Police Inspector Jones ______ 27 (interview) four 'Santa Claus' suspects. He ______ 28 (have) three questions for each of them.

3 **Vervollständigen Sie die Antworten der Verdächtigen auf die Fragen des Inspektors.**

Where were you, and what were you doing at 9 a.m. this morning?

1. I __________ at home. I __________ breakfast. (be; have)

2. I __________ in my car. I __________ into town. (be; drive)

3. I __________ on Ott Street. I __________ a bell. (stand; ring)

4. I __________ on Ott Street. I __________ a bell. (stand; ring)

Did anyone see you?

5. Yes, my wife __________ me. She __________ for work at 9.05. (see; leave)

6. Yes, a hitchhiker ______________ me.
He ______________ my car at about 8.45. (see; stop)

7. Yes, two people ______________ money to me. (give)

8. Yes. About fifteen people ______________ me at 9.00. (see)

Nach diesen Interviews verhaftet Inspektor Jones einen der Santas. Wer ist der Dieb?

1.3 Das *simple past* und das *present perfect*

Read the examples

❶ Rudi Schmidt from Cologne, Germany, **came** to Iowa last September as an exchange student.
❷ Rudi **has been** in Iowa now **for** about two months, **since** September 3rd.
❸ Rudi **has lost** his money. Now he can't take the bus.
❹ He **has** already **learned** a lot about the American way of life, but he **has** never **been** at a Halloween party.

Remember

Das ***simple past*** wird für Handlungen verwendet, die zu einer bestimmten erwähnten oder bekannten Zeit passierten, eindeutig in der Vergangenheit abgeschlossen wurden und keinen direkten Bezug zur Gegenwart haben ❶.

Das ***present perfect*** wird verwendet:

- für Vorgänge, die in der Vergangenheit angefangen haben und noch andauern, oft mit for (bei Angabe eines Zeitraums) oder since (bei Angabe eines Zeitpunkts) (siehe auch **Abschnitt 1.4 Das *present perfect progressive***) ❷,
- für vergangene Vorgänge, deren Auswirkungen auf die Gegenwart betont werden sollen (der Zeitpunkt des eigentlichen Vorgangs ist unwichtig und wird nicht genannt; wichtig ist nur der Bezug zur Gegenwart) ❸,
- oft mit folgenden Signalwörtern: ever, never, recently, lately, just, already, yet, die diese Brücke zwischen Vergangenheit und Gegenwart verdeutlichen ❹.

4 Rudi Schmidt, ein deutscher Austauschschüler, unterhält sich mit amerikanischen Mitschülern.

Vervollständigen Sie das Gespräch. Wenn kein Verb angegeben ist, ergänzen Sie den Satz mit einer Kurzantwort (have/haven't).

Tom: Hi, Meg, *have you met* 1 (meet) Rudi yet? He's our new exchange student from Germany.

Meg: No, I ______ 2. Pleased to meet you. How long ______ 3 (you/be) in Iowa?

Rudi: I ______ 4 (come) at the beginning of September.

Rachel: Hi, guys! ______ 5 (you/hear) about the Halloween party this evening?

Rudi: Halloween? How do you celebrate Halloween?

Meg: You mean, you ______ 6 (never/be) to a Halloween party?

Rudi: No, I ______ 7.

Meg: It's a night of witches, ghosts and goblins (= Kobold). Kids dress up in costumes and go to their neighbours 'trick-or-treating'. That means, the neighbour must give them a treat, or little present, or the children have the right to play a trick (= Scherz) on them.

Tom: And you make 'jack-o-lanterns'. That's a hollowed-out pumpkin (= Kürbis) with a face cut into it, and with a candle inside. I ______ 8 (have) one myself every Halloween since I was eight. And I ________ [9] (already/make) five jack-o-lanterns for the party this evening.

Rudi: Is Halloween always on October 31st?

Meg: Yes – at least it ________ [10] (be) ever since I can remember.

Rudi: Do you celebrate All Saints' Day (= Allerheiligen)?

Meg: What's that? I ________ [11] (never/hear) of it.

Tom: Actually, many years ago, in England, originally there ________ [12] (be) a connection between Halloween and All Saints' Day. November 1st ________ [13] (be) a day for honouring the good spirits, and legend said that the night before ________ [14] (be) the time for evil spirits. But most people in America ________ [15] (forget) the connection.

Rachel: Actually, All Saints' Day is a huge festival in Mexico, even with family picnics at the cemeteries (= Friedhof).

Rudi: ________ [16] (you/ever/be) to Mexico, Rachel?

Rachel: Yes, I ________ [17]. I ________ [18] (go) there two years ago with my family. It ________ [19] (be) a fantastic vacation. Oh, here's the waiter! I ________ [20] (not/decide/yet) what I want to eat. Where's the menu?

5 Im folgenden Gespräch finden Sie weitere Fragen und Antworten zu Feiertagen und Festen.

Welche sind grammatikalisch falsch? Schreiben Sie die richtigen Zeiten daneben.

1. Have you ever been to the Oktoberfest? ________
2. Yes, I have been there two years ago. ________
3. But I haven't enjoyed the Oktoberfest very much then. ________
4. I've experienced Easter in Italy. ________
5. It was fascinating. ________
6. My brother was in Germany since last July. ________
7. He went to a wine festival on the Rhine last August. ________

1.4 Das *present perfect progressive*

Read the examples

❶ They**'ve been celebrating** their wedding **for** two days now.
❷ She**'s been working** at the Christmas bazaar **since** 10 a.m.
❸ How long **has** that turkey **been roasting**?
❹ I **haven't believed** in Santa Claus since I was five.

Remember

Das ***present perfect progressive*** betont die Dauer eines Vorgangs, der in der Vergangenheit angefangen hat und noch nicht abgeschlossen ist ❶-❸.
Beachten Sie: Im Deutschen verwendet man dafür die Gegenwart:
Ich wohne hier (schon) seit sieben Jahren. = I've been living here for seven years.

Dieser andauernde Zeitraum wird mit since („seit" bezogen auf einen Zeitpunkt) oder for („seit" bezogen auf einen Zeitraum) gekennzeichnet ❶ ❷.

Verben, die keine Handlungsverben sind, die Meinungen (z. B. believe, think), Sinneswahrnehmungen (z. B. see, smell, taste), Besitz (z. B. have), Sein (z. B. exist, be), Zuneigung/Abneigung (z. B. (dis)like, love, prefer, hate) und Wollen (z. B. want) ausdrücken, werden in der Regel nicht in der *progressive form* verwendet ❹.

6 Die folgenden Sätze enthalten Informationen über Feiertage in England und in den USA.

Vervollständigen Sie die Sätze mit dem passenden Verb im *present perfect progressive* und setzen Sie since oder for mit der Zeitangabe ein.

eat *enjoy* *fill* *hold* *hide* *listen* *sell* *stand* ~~*steam*~~ *walk*

1. It's a few weeks before Christmas in England, and Mrs Smyth's plum pudding *has been steaming for* ten hours.
2. Mr Smyth ______ in a queue at the post office with his Christmas parcels ______ 45 minutes.
3. American children ______ to the poem 'Twas the Night before Christmas' by Clement Moore every Christmas ______ 1822.

4. It's 3 a.m. on December 25th, and Santa Claus ______ stockings at the Jones' house ______ a few minutes.
5. It's only February, but the shops ______ chocolate Easter eggs and rabbits ______ a few weeks.
6. It's Easter, and the Easter bunny ______ eggs in the garden ______ early this morning.
7. American children ______ the costumes and pranks (= Streiche) at Halloween ever ______ immigrants brought the tradition over many years ago.
8. It's the evening of October 31st now, and Halloween 'ghosts' ______ through the neighbourhood ______ 5 p.m.
9. Americans ______ turkey, sweet potatoes, cranberries and pumpkin pie on Thanksgiving Day in November ever ______ the Pilgrim Fathers did it in 1620.
10. On Memorial Day, the last Monday in May, they ______ a big car race, the Indy 500, in Indianapolis, USA, ______ many years.

7 Übersetzen Sie die fehlenden Satzteile.

1. ______ a suitable present for his mother. (Seit heute Morgen sucht er ...)
2. ______ those terrible Christmas songs? (Seit wann spielen deine Nachbarn ...)
3. – He's at home writing Valentine cards to all his girlfriends. – Really? ______ ? (Wie lange macht er das schon?)
4. We're planning a big family celebration for next week. My parents ______ . (... sind seit 50 Jahren verheiratet.)

5. __________ 'A Christmas Carol' by Charles Dickens __________. (Seit letzter Woche lese ich ...)

8 Carol schreibt an eine Freundin und berichtet von verschiedenen Feiern in der Vergangenheit und Gegenwart.

Setzen Sie in ihren Brief die richtigen Verbformen ein – *simple past, present perfect* oder *present perfect progressive*.

Dear Sigrid,

What lovely news that you can come for the Easter holidays! Mom and dad were [1] (be) *delighted, too. Easter is always spring-cleaning time around here, and they* __________ [2] (clean) *like crazy since yesterday. I* __________ [3] (wash) *windows for two hours yesterday afternoon! So the house will be clean for you. Last year we* __________ [4] (hide) *Easter eggs in the garden for my little brothers, but this year they* __________ [5] (tell) *us for weeks now that they know there's no Easter Bunny, so we shouldn't bother with the eggs. I* __________ *already* __________ [6] (paint) *a lot of them anyway, so we'll have a lot to eat.*

You remember my Aunt Meg and Uncle Harry, don't you? They __________ *just* __________ [7] (celebrate) *their 25th wedding anniversary. My parents* __________ [8] (not give) *them a present yet, because for weeks Meg and Harry* __________ [9] (tell) *everybody not to. But last night my parents* __________ [10] (decide) *to give them a weekend in London. My aunt* __________ [11] (want) *to go there for years, but they* __________ *never* __________ [12] (manage). *We thought you might arrange theatre tickets for them. Could you please bring the current programmes with you?*

See you next week.

Love, ***Carol***

1.5 Das Futur: *will, going to, simple present, present progressive*

Read the examples

1. The party **will be** a huge success. We'**ll** probably **go** to it.
2. I imagine Stella **will want** to take her holidays in June this year.
3. I don't know, but I'**ll call** her and find out.
4. She'**ll be** 37 years old next month.
5. He'**s going to live** in China for a year.
6. Look at those clouds! It'**s going to rain** soon.
7. The school **is having** a reception (= Empfang) for him this Saturday.
8. The reception **begins** at 5 p.m.

Remember

Das ***will-future*** wird verwendet:

- ▷ für Vermutungen und Vorhersagen, häufig in Verbindung mit Adverbien wie maybe, probably ❶ oder mit Verben wie believe, imagine, suppose, think, be sure ❷,
- ▷ zum Ausdruck einer spontanen Entscheidung oder eines Angebots ❸,
- ▷ zum Ausdruck nicht beeinflussbarer Tatsachen mit Bezug auf die Zukunft ❹.

Das ***going to-future*** drückt aus:

- ▷ selbst bestimmbare feste Absichten und Pläne ❺,
- ▷ ein nahe bevorstehendes Ereignis, das man schon durch bestimmte Vorzeichen voraussehen kann ❻.

Das ***present progressive*** kann anstatt des *going to-future* für feste Pläne in der nahen Zukunft verwendet werden, wenn diese schon für einen bestimmten Zeitpunkt vereinbart sind ❼.
Das ***simple present*** verwendet man oftmals für planmäßige Vorgänge (Fahrpläne, Stundenpläne usw.) in Verbindung mit einer Zeitangabe ❽.

Beachten Sie: Diese Regeln geben die bevorzugte Verwendung der verschiedenen Zeitformen für künftiges Geschehen wieder. Abweichungen davon sind aber im aktiven Gebrauch möglich, da die Zeitform von der Absicht des Sprechers abhängt.

9 Nach vielen Dienstjahren geht der Lehrer Peter Johnson in Pension. Aus diesem Anlass gibt es einen Empfang, auf dem Mr Johnson seine Pläne für seinen nicht so ruhigen Ruhestand mitteilt.

Setzen Sie folgende Ausdrücke in die Einladung ein:

are invited *will be* *will be provided*

There ______________ [1] *a reception*

honouring Mr Peter Johnson on the occasion of his retirement,

in the school assembly hall on Friday, June 7, at 6 p.m.

All faculty, staff and students of Mr Johnson

______________ [2] *to attend.*

Light refreshments ______________ [3].

10 Folgender Dialog findet auf Mr Johnsons Abschiedsfest statt.

Streichen Sie die weniger passenden Verbformen durch.

1. Congratulations, Mr Johnson! Do you think you ~~miss~~/~~are missing~~/will miss teaching English after all these years?
2. I believe I am going to miss/am missing/will miss my colleagues and students. But actually, I am continuing/am going to continue/will continue teaching English – just in a different way.
3. Really? What are you going to do/do you do/will you do?
4. My wife and I are going to live/live/will live in China for a year, and I am going to teach/teach/will teach English at the University of Peking. In fact, we are going to leave/leave/will leave on August 1st by ship. Our tour is stopping/stops/will stop in Egypt and India on the way.
5. Are you going to sell/Do you sell/Will you sell your house?

11 Auch Gerlinde Schmidt wird bald ein Jahr lang im Ausland leben, als Austauschstudentin in Australien.

Ergänzen Sie diesen Brief, der über eine Party für Gerlinde berichtet, mit einer passenden Zukunftsform des Verbs.

Dear Trudy,

We *are having* [1] *(have) a farewell party for Gerlinde this Saturday evening at my house at 8 p.m. She* ______ [2] *(leave) for Australia next week. I believe she* ______ [3] *(live) there for one year as an exchange student. Can you come? I* ______ [4] *(make) potato salad if you bring sausages. Thomas and Robert* ______ [5] *(bring) drinks. I* ______ [6] *(call) you tomorrow.*

Hilde

12 Auf Gerlindes Party hören Sie folgendes Gespräch.

Übersetzen Sie die fehlenden Satzteile.

1. *Are you going to live with* a family? (Wirst du ... wohnen?)
2. Yes. ______ next week at the airport. (Sie holen mich ab ...)
3. ______ ? (Wann fliegst du?)
4. ______ (Mein Flugzeug fliegt ab) on Sunday at 10 p.m., and ______ (landet) in Sydney on Monday at 6 p.m.
5. I suppose that you ______ on the way. (... viele Bücher lesen wirst)
6. Right! ______ English textbooks and try to polish up my English. (Ich werde ... lesen)

1.6 Das *future progressive* und das *future perfect*

Read the examples

1. At this time next week, Mr Johnson **will be travelling** to China.
2. At the end of two years, the Johnsons **will have learned** a lot about the Chinese way of life.

Remember

Das ***future progressive*** (will + be + *-ing-form*) wird verwendet, um auszudrücken, dass etwas zu einer bestimmten Zeit in der Zukunft gerade vor sich gehen wird ❶.

Das ***future perfect*** (will + have + *past participle*) wird verwendet, um auszudrücken, dass ein Vorgang zu einem bestimmten Zeitpunkt in der Zukunft abgeschlossen sein wird ❷.

13 Peter Johnson und Gerlinde Schmidt werden bald für eine längere Zeit ins Ausland gehen - Peter nach China und Gerlinde nach Australien. Ihre Aufenthalte werden von verschiedenen Organisationen finanziert und beide haben einen typischen Brief bekommen, der sie auf die Verhältnisse in ihrem Austauschland vorbereiten soll.

a) **Vervollständigen Sie Peter Johnsons Orientierungsbrief mit dem *future progressive* oder *future perfect*.**

... You will be living 1 (live) in three-room flats provided by the university for faculty (= Dozenten). These are presently under construction (= im Bau), but the university assured us that by the time you arrive they ______ 2 (be finished). They ______ 3 (be furnished) by that time, as well. You ______ 4 (teach) four classes daily. The exact level has not yet been confirmed, but hopefully the university ______ 5 (decide) this by the end of May, so that we can pass on the information to you. You mentioned that your wife ______ 6 (write) a book on Chinese embroidery (= Stickerei) while she is in China. I hear that by the end of December, the new centre for handicrafts (= Handarbeit) in Peking ______ 7 (open), and I'm sure that the staff there will be glad to give her any information they can. I'm glad to hear that you ______ 8 (get) a minimum knowledge of the Chinese language before you go. Of course, you ______ 9 (take) a Chinese course

at the university as well, and better yet, while you're in China, ________ [10] (get) a lot of first-hand practice. Let us know if you or Mrs Johnson have any more questions.

All the best

John Hailey

b) **Vervollständigen Sie Gerlinde Schmidts Orientierungsbrief mit dem *future progressive* oder *future perfect*.**

... You ________ [1] (live) with the Thomas White family in Sydney. Their address is on the enclosed information sheet, and they ________ [2] (get) in touch with (= Kontakt aufnehmen) you in the next few days.

They ________ [3] (expect) you to keep the same rules they have for their own children. The oldest daughter Sharon ________ [4] (study) German at school while you are there, and is delighted that you ________ [5] (give) her first-hand practice now and then.

You ________ [6] (attend) classes at Northside High School, and ________ [7] (participate) in the afternoon school sports or activities of your choice. There is also a prospectus of the school enclosed.

We understand that by the time you leave for your exchange year, you ________ [8] (complete) all coursework and examinations for your German 11th class.

It's clear that you ________ [9] (receive) the vaccinations (= Impfung) necessary for European travellers to Australia. We also understand that you ________ [10] (complete) payment of the handling fee (= Gebühr) as stated in the previous letter. Should you have any further questions, do not hesitate to write and ask.

Yours sincerely,

Mary Richards
Director of International Student Exchange Program

1.7 Das *past perfect*, das *past perfect progressive* und das *future in the past*

Read the examples

❶ Last week, Martha gave a birthday party for Jenny and **had planned** everything very carefully.
❷ She **had been telling** her friends all week that it **would be** the best party of the year.
❸ The party **was going to be** a surprise for Jenny.

Remember

Das ***past perfect*** wird verwendet, wenn in der Vergangenheit zwei Handlungen aufeinanderfolgten. Die Handlung, die zeitlich voranging, steht im *past perfect*, die darauffolgende Handlung im *simple past* ❶.

Beim ***past perfect progressive*** (had + be + *-ing-form*) liegt wie bei allen *progressive forms* die Betonung auf der Dauer und dem Ablauf der Handlung. Es wird verwendet, um Vorgänge zu beschreiben, die bis zu einem bestimmten Zeitpunkt in der Vergangenheit noch andauerten ❷.

Das ***future in the past*** (was/were going to + Verb oder would + Verb) wird verwendet, um von einem Punkt in der Vergangenheit aus über die Zukunft zu sprechen ❷ ❸.

14 Martha hatte für Jennys Geburtstagsfeier alles sorgfältig geplant und war sicher, dass sie ein Riesenerfolg werden würde. Aber es wurde eine Katastrophe!

Lesen Sie Marthas Notizzettel durch und schreiben Sie auf, was sie vor Beginn des Festes erledigt und nicht erledigt hatte.

- *make chocolate cake*
- ✔ *buy present*
- ✔ *decorate the party room*
- *borrow extra chairs from the neighbours*
- ✔ *order flowers*
- ✔ *make salads*

1. *Martha hadn't made* a chocolate cake.
2. *She* ______ a present.
3. ______ the party room.
4. ______ extra chairs from the neighbours.
5. ______ flowers.
6. ______ salads.

15 Aber viele Dinge sind bei Marthas Party anders gelaufen als geplant.

Vervollständigen Sie die Sätze mit einem Verb im *future in the past*.

bring *carry over* *come* *have* ~~*make*~~ *surprise*

1. Tony *was going to make* a carrot cake, but he didn't have any carrots.
2. Mark ______ CDs, but he brought cassettes instead.
3. Martha ______ lots of flowers for the party, but the delivery service went on strike.
4. Mary ______ alone, but she brought four guests, who were all unfriendly.
5. Tom and Jerry ______ the drinks, but they dropped the bottles on the way and they all broke.

16 Im Gegensatz zu Martha hatte Jeff für sein Fest letzte Woche fast nichts vorbereitet.

Ergänzen Sie die Sätze mit dem *past perfect progressive*.

Jeff hadn't prepared for his party because ...

1. he *hadn't been feeling* (not feel) very well.
2. he ______ (study) for his exams.
3. he ______ (pack) his backpack for a big trekking holiday.
4. his cousin from the USA ______ (visit) him.
5. he ______ (repair) his old car.

17 Es gab aber bei Jeffs Fest viele angenehme Überraschungen und es wurde ein Riesenerfolg.

Vervollständigen Sie die Sätze mit einem Verb im *future in the past*.

be *cook* ~~*play*~~ *show* *sing*

Jeff had no idea that ...

1. Jack *was going to play* the guitar.
2. Jack and his girlfriend ______ so beautifully.
3. Susan and Tom ______ Chinese food for the party.
4. Rip ______ wonderful photos of his trip to Nepal.
5. Everybody ______ in such a good mood.

2 DAS PASSIV

Thema: Changes in Small Town, USA

Read the examples

➊	Subjekt	Form von *be*	Partizip Perfekt	
simple present:	Old buildings	**are**	**torn down**	too often.
present progressive:	Our church	**is being**	**torn down**	at this moment.
simple past:	It	**was**	**built**	in 1764 by Wren.
present perfect:	God	**has been**	**worshipped**	there for centuries.
will-future:	A modern church	**will be**	**built**	in its place.
Modale Hilfsverben:	Something	**should be**	**done**	about such crimes.

➋ **It is said** that many old bridges are too weak.

Remember

- ▷ Das Passiv wird wie im Deutschen verwendet, wenn wichtiger ist, **was** getan wird, und weniger wichtig ist, wer es getan hat. Das Passiv wird mit der passenden Zeitform von be und dem Partizip Perfekt gebildet. Die Regeln für die zu wählende Zeitform unterscheiden sich nicht vom Aktiv. So müssen Handlungen, die gerade vor sich gehen, – wie im Aktiv – in der *progressive form* stehen, die im Passiv mit being gebildet wird. Ein Handelnder wird (nach by) nur dann erwähnt, wenn er für den Zusammenhang von Interesse ist ➊.
- ▷ Bei Verben wie believe, consider, expect, know, report, say, think kann man eine Passivkonstruktion mit It is ... that bilden, um das unpersönliche „man“ (man erwartet/sagt ...) auszudrücken ➋.

1 Vervollständigen Sie die folgenden Sätze mit den entsprechenden Passivformen.

1. A lot *has been written* (write) about famous American cities like New York.
2. But ______ the average foreigner ______ (inform) about how small towns in the USA ______ (change) over the years?
3. In small towns in the Midwest, many developments wouldn't ______ (dream) of 100 years ago.
4. Perhaps a hundred years ago, German, French or Italian ______ (speak) by the older generations.
5. These days, foreign languages ______ always ______ (not require) for school, but if students want to learn one, Spanish ______ (teach) most often.
6. Many family-owned restaurants ______ (close) down, and in their place, restaurants belonging to huge national chains (= Kette) ______ (open).
7. Perhaps these ______ (replace) by more individual restaurants again sometime in the future.
8. Two-lane roads ______ (transform) into 4- or 6-lane highways.
9. Even these roads ______ (enlarge) constantly these days.
10. Older homes in the town centres ______ often ______ (neglect) and many ______ (tear) down as middle class families have headed for the suburbs.
11. These days, some of these fine old homes ______ (restore), but they ______ (not care) for as they should be afterwards.
12. As television became more and more common in the 1950s, many cinemas in small towns ______ (close).
13. Of course, many improvements ______ (make) in American towns over the years, as well.

14. Schools and hospitals ______ (modernize).
15. Perhaps the problems of pollution and neglect ______ (balance) by the technological advances that make people's lives safer and more comfortable.

2 Ein Kleinstadtpolitiker hält eine Rede und beschwert sich über die Zustände, die die Regierungspartei verursacht hat. Er verspricht auch viele Reformen. Dabei ist er aber sehr diplomatisch und nennt seine Gegner nicht.

Übersetzen Sie die fehlenden Teile seiner Rede.

1. Man hat die wichtigsten Denkmäler unserer Stadt vernichtet.
   The most important monuments of our town *have been destroyed*.
2. Erst vor zehn Jahren wurden die letzten Beispiele des Baustils aus der Zeit vor dem Bürgerkrieg von einem Kunsthistoriker entdeckt.
   Just ten years ago, the last examples of pre-Civil War architecture ______ ______ by an art historian.
3. Trotz seiner und meiner Empfehlungen wurden diese immer noch nicht instand gesetzt (renovate).
   In spite of his and my recommendations, these ______.
4. Gerade in diesen Tagen wird das Escher-Haus in der Poplar Street abgerissen; ein Parkhaus wird stattdessen errichtet.
   Even now, the Escher House on Poplar Street ______; a garage ______ in its place.
5. Kriminalität wird hier nicht als ein echtes Problem anerkannt (recognize).
   Crime ______ as a real problem.
6. Aber jedes Jahr werden Hunderte von Jugendlichen von Drogenhändlern verführt (corrupt).
   But every year hundreds of our young people ______ by drug dealers.

7. Man sagt, dass sich unser Klima ändert.

_______________ that our climate is changing.

8. Aber es werden im Moment keine Umweltreformen durchgeführt (carry out).

But at the moment, no environmental reforms _______________ .

9. Wenn ich gewählt werde (elect), wird diese Stadt zu einem schönen, einem sicheren Ort gemacht.

If I _______________ , this city _______________ _______ into a beautiful and safe place.

3 DIE INDIREKTE REDE

Thema: A visit from a difficult prime minister

Read the examples

❶	The President's secretary: "The Prime Minister of Zandia **wants** money for an irrigation project." The secretary **said** the PM **wanted** money for an irrigation project.	simple present ▼ simple past
❷	The secretary: "The PM **is coming** for a visit in three days." The secretary **said** the PM **was coming** for a visit three days later.	present progressive ▼ past progressive
❸	A minister: "The PM **has asked** several countries for aid." The minister **told me (that)** the PM **had asked** several countries for aid.	present perfect ▼ past perfect
❹	A minister: "They **didn't give** it to him." The minister **said** they **hadn't given** it to him.	simple past ▼ past perfect
❺	A minister: "**Will you give** him more money?" The minister **asked whether I would give** him more money.	will ▼ would
❻	The President: "**I can't risk** losing **our** bases in Zandia." The President **insisted** (that) **he couldn't risk** losing **their** bases in Zandia.	can ▼ could

Remember

Wenn in der indirekten Rede das einleitende Verb in der Vergangenheit steht, werden in der indirekten Rede andere Zeitformen als in der direkten Rede verwendet. Die Zeitform der direkten Rede verschiebt sich um eine „Zeitstufe" zurück *(back shift)* ❶–❻.

That kann nach dem einleitenden Verb meist weggelassen werden ❹.
Die Wortstellung bleibt bei Fragesätzen in der direkten Rede die gleiche wie bei Aussagesätzen. Wenn die direkte Rede kein Fragewort enthält, steht if oder whether in der indirekten Rede ❺.

Beachten Sie: Nach tell und inform steht vor Namen oder Pronomen nie to ❸.

Wie im Deutschen muss man immer bedenken, dass aus der Sicht des Berichtenden Angaben zu Ort, Zeit und Personen anders als in der direkten Rede ausgedrückt werden müssen ❷ ❺ ❻.

1 Für das Treffen des Premierministers von Zandia mit dem Präsidenten eines mächtigen Landes werden Vorbereitungen getroffen. Der Präsident führt ein Gespräch mit seinem engsten Berater. Die Sekretärin ist aber eine Agentin und berichtet einem Vertrauten des Premierministers von Zandia nachher, was gesagt wurde.

Ergänzen Sie ihren Bericht und beginnen Sie jede indirekte Rede mit:

asked *asked* *claimed* *had no idea* *informed* *insisted* *said* *said* ~~*was surprised*~~ *wondered*

1. "What? The Prime Minister is coming again so soon? That's a surprise!"
   The President *was surprised* that the Prime Minister *was coming* again so soon.
2. "Is the Prime Minister going to come alone?"
   He ______
   whether the Prime Minister ______ come alone.
3. "We must have two of our interpreters, not just their interpreters, at the meeting."
   The President ______ that they ______
   ______ two of ______ interpreters at the meeting, and not just ______ interpreters.
4. "Does the Prime Minister expect a loan from us?"
   The President ______
   ______ if the Prime Minister ______
   a loan (= Darlehen).

5. "How much will he want, I wonder?"

The President ______ ______ how much he ______ .

6. "The Prime Minister gave 10,000 guns to the neighbouring country of Bandia."

An adviser (= Berater) ______ the President that the Prime Minister ______ the neighbouring country of Bandia 10,000 guns.

7. "Really? Are they really allies?"

The President ______ that ______ really allies.

8. "I've been negotiating (= verhandeln) with Bandia to give us more bases (= Stützpunkt)."

The President ______ that he ______ with Bandia to give ______ more bases.

9. "Bandia certainly didn't seem too friendly toward Zandia last time I talked to them."

The President ______ that Bandia ______ too friendly towards Zandia last time ______ to them.

10. "We'll only give them more money if they threaten to take away our bases."

He ______ that ______ more money if ______ to take away ______ bases.

2 Eine Woche später berichtet der Premierminister seinen Ministern von seinem Gespräch mit dem Präsidenten.

Vervollständigen Sie die indirekte Rede und ändern Sie dabei die unterstrichenen Wörter.

1. "We received news of your visit three days ago."

   He said *they had received news of our visit three days before* .

2. "What can we do to keep good relations with your country?"

   He asked what ______ ______ to keep good relations with ______ country.

3. "Have you been informed of these reports of Zandian guns in Bandia?"

   He asked whether ______ of ______ reports of Zandian guns in Bandia.

4. "We received them just five days ago."

   He told me ______ them just five days ______ .

5. "I'm glad to hear that relations between Bandia and your country are good."

   He insisted that ______ glad to hear that relations between Bandia and ______ country ______ ______ good.

6. "We'll transfer the money to your central bank tomorrow."

   He promised that ______ ______ the money to ______ central bank ______ .

4 IF-SÄTZE

Thema: Second hand

4.1 Typ 1 und Typ 2

Read the examples

1. **If** you **don't need** that old thing, **sell** it at a flea market.
2. **If** you **sell** it, you **can use** the money for something else.
3. **If** you**'re** lucky, you **will get** a good price for it.
4. **If** I **had** more money, I **could buy** expensive clothes.
5. **If** I **were** smarter, I **might be** rich.
6. **If** you **sold** your piano, you **would have** much more room.

Remember

Typ 1	if + *simple present*	will/can + *infinitive/imperative*
Typ 2	if + *simple past*	would/could/might + *infinitive*

In *if*-Sätzen, in denen das Verb im *if*-Teil im ***simple present*** steht (Typ 1), nennt der Sprecher eine **Bedingung**, die aus seiner Sicht **erfüllbar** ist. Im Hauptsatz steht dann die Folge, also was passieren wird, wenn die Bedingung erfüllt ist:

- ▷ mit Imperativ (als bedingter Ratschlag) ❶,
- ▷ mit Hilfsverb (z. B. can als bedingte Möglichkeit) ❷,
- ▷ mit will (als wahrscheinliche Folge) ❸.

In *if*-Sätzen, in denen das Verb im *if*-Teil im ***simple past*** steht (Typ 2), nennt der Sprecher eine **Bedingung**, deren Erfüllung aus seiner Sicht **unwahrscheinlich** ❹ ist oder deren Erfüllung **unmöglich** ❺ ist, oder es handelt sich um vorgestellte Situationen ❻.

Beachten Sie: Will und would stehen nie im *if*-Teil des Satzes! (Ausnahme would like*:* If you would like to leave now, ...)

In *if*-Sätzen des 2. Typs *(simple past)* heißt die Form von to be für die 1. und 3. Person Singular eigentlich were (I/he/she/it were), obwohl sich was im gesprochenen Englisch immer mehr durchsetzt.

1. Wenn eine Lampe vom Flohmarkt sprechen könnte, könnte sie eine interessante Geschichte erzählen!

Vervollständigen Sie diese Dialoge mit *if*-Sätzen des Typs 1.

(at home)

Mother: There are just too many things in your room. If you *don't need* 1 (not/need) this lamp any more, ______ 2 (give) it to Tom.

Daughter: All right. If Tom ______ 3 (not/need) it, he ______ 4 (sell) it at a flea market (= Flohmarkt).

(at the flea market)

Man: Does this lamp work?

Tom: It ______ 5 (work) fine if you ______ 6 (put) a new plug (= Stecker) on it.

Man: OK. I ______ 7 (give) you $10 for it if you ______ 8 (give) me that Chinese vase with it.

(at home)

Wife: If that lamp ______ 9 (come) in our living room, I ______ 10 (leave) you, George!

Man: Well, all right, if you ______ 11 (feel) so strongly about it, I ______ 12 (give) it to Aunt Martha for her birthday.

2 Vervollständigen Sie den restlichen Dialog mit *if*-Sätzen des Typs 2.

Wife: If you *gave* 1 (give) that lamp to Aunt Martha for her birthday, she ______ 2 (never/forgive) you.

Man: What if I ______ 3 (include) this Chinese vase?

Wife: She ______ 4 (break) it over your head!

Man: Well, if the flea market ______ 5 (be) still open, maybe I ______ 6 (sell) it again. But it's closed. If I ______ 7 (take) you out for dinner, ______ you ______ 8 (forgive) me?

Wife: Of course, dear.

3 Übersetzen Sie diese Sätze.

1. Wenn ich mehr Geld hätte, würde ich nur neue Autos kaufen.

   If I had more money, I

2. Wenn ich nur neue Autos hätte, hätte ich weniger Reparaturen.

3. Wenn ich weniger Reparaturen hätte, hätte ich mehr Geld.

4.2 Typ 3

Read the examples

❶ **If** they **had realized** the painting was worth so much money, they **wouldn't have** sold it.

❷ They **might have bought** it **if** the price **had been** right.

Remember

Typ 3	if + *past perfect*	would/could/might + have + *past participle*

In *if*-Sätzen, in denen das Verb im *if*-Teil im *past perfect* steht (Typ 3), nennt der Sprecher eine **Bedingung**, deren Erfüllung **nicht mehr möglich** ist, da das Beschriebene schon passiert ist. Im Hauptsatz steht, was gewesen wäre, wenn ...

Beachten Sie:
Ich hätte es gekauft = I **would have bought** it.
Wenn ich es gekauft hätte = If I **had bought** it.

4 Ein Gemälde, das über 40 Jahre unbeachtet in einer schottischen Kirche lag, wurde von einem Kunsthändler entdeckt und zu dem Auktionshaus *Christie's* geschickt. Hier wurde es als ein Werk des italienischen Malers Mattia Preti identifiziert und für 825.000 £ verkauft.

Lesen Sie den Text und vervollständigen Sie die Sätze.

1. If someone in the church *had noticed* (notice) the value of the painting, it ______ (might/be sold) earlier.
2. If the art dealer ______ (not/come) to the church by chance, he ______ (not/see) the painting.
3. If he ______ (not/take) the painting to *Christie's*, it ______ (not/be) identified as a painting by Preti.
4. If I ______ (be) the pastor of that Scottish church, I ______ (be) very angry.
5. If the painting ______ (be painted) by me, it ______ (not/be sold) for £825,000!

5 Eine Puppe, die im Jahre 1909 von *Kammer & Reinhart* in Deutschland hergestellt worden war, lag jahrelang unbeachtet im Schaufenster eines Trödelladens (second-hand shop). Sie wurde für wenig Geld erstanden, später aber für 24.000 $ verkauft.

Übersetzen Sie die fehlenden Satzteile.

1. If the doll ______ by *Kammer & Reinhart*, it wouldn't have brought so much money. (... nicht von ... hergestellt wäre, ...)
2. If the owner had known its value, ______.
   (... hätte er die Puppe nicht zum Trödler gebracht.)
3. The doll might have landed in the trash ______.
   (... wenn niemand sie erkannt und gekauft hätte.)

5 MODALE HILFSVERBEN

Thema: Professional life

Wie im Deutschen können Sie Sprechabsichten ausdrücken durch die Zusammenstellung von Verben mit entsprechenden modalen Hilfsverben. Da einige dieser Hilfsverben nur ein oder zwei Zeitformen haben, werden in bestimmten Fällen Ersatzformen mit ähnlicher Bedeutung benutzt, z. B. must und have to.

Hier eine Übersicht über einige der wichtigsten modalen Hilfsverben:

Fähigkeit/Möglichkeit	can, be able to
Erlaubnis	can , may, could, be allowed to
Angebot	shall, can, should
Notwendigkeit	must, have (got) to, needn't
Ratschlag/Aufforderung	ought to, should, had better, be to, be supposed to
Annahme/Wahrscheinlichkeit	must be, may be, might be, could be, is said to be, is supposed to be, is considered to be
Frühere Gewohnheit/Zustand	used to be
„an etwas gewöhnt sein"	be used to + -ing-Form

Wie Sie sehen, kann ein modales Hilfsverb verschiedene Sprechabsichten ausdrücken. So kann z. B. auch das deutsche modale Hilfsverb „sollen" nicht immer mit shall oder should übersetzt werden. Man muss die Sprechintention bedenken und das passende englische modale Hilfsverb wählen.

5.1 Fähigkeit/Möglichkeit: *can, be able to*

Read the examples

1. Ashley **can** do most secretarial work very well.
2. She **is** especially **able to** deal cleverly with customer problems.
3. Two months ago her boss told her that they **couldn't** afford to keep her.
4. Ashley **wasn't able to** convince them that they needed her.
5. Since then she **hasn't been able to** find a new job.
6. Now she has several interviews coming up and she **might be able** to find an even better job.

5 MODALE HILFSVERBEN

Remember

Can (not) und could (not) drücken eine allgemeine Fähigkeit ❶ (oder Unfähigkeit) bzw. Möglichkeit (oder Unmöglichkeit) ❸ aus.

Be able to wird selten in der Gegenwart benutzt, kann aber besondere Fähigkeiten betonen ❷. In der Vergangenheit wird es bevorzugt, um zu zeigen, dass man (nicht) in der Lage war, etwas zu machen oder zu schaffen ❹.

Man verwendet ausschließlich (not) be able to für *future*, *present perfect* und *past perfect* sowie zusammen mit anderen modalen Hilfsverben ❺ ❻.

1 Ashley spricht mit einer Freundin über ein Vorstellungsgespräch, das sie bald bei einer Firma haben wird.

Vervollständigen Sie ihre Sätze mit der passendsten Form von can, could oder be able to.

1. I ________ go there for an interview next Thursday.
2. They ________ tell me much about the job on the phone yesterday.
3. I hope John will ________ drive me there because the bus is always late.
4. They do a lot of business with Spain. Unfortunately, I ________ speak Spanish.
5. Do you think I ________ to convince them I'm the right person for the job?
6. Perhaps it's a bit late, but I really ________ apply for the job earlier.
7. I haven't ________ get any other job interviews up to now.

Dies hat der Personalchef zu Ashley gesagt:

8. ________ you use Excel und Photoshop?
9. Do you think you would ________ work from home two days a week?

10. ______ you do a few tests for us next week?

11. ______ you speak any other foreign languages?

12. Have you ______ to get any experience in marketing?

13. When would you ______ start work?

14. Would you ______ do a business trip now and then?

15. We might ______ give you an office of your own.

5.2 Erlaubnis: *can , may, could, be allowed to*
Angebot: *shall, can, should*

Read the examples

❶ Susan, it's your living room. **Can** I smoke in here?
❷ Excuse me, sir, **am** I **allowed to** smoke in here?
❸ At the moment it's okay, but from next week on you **won't be allowed to**.
❹ **May** I have some of this coffee, Mr. Jones?
❺ **Could** I possibly have some of those biscuits, too?
❻ **Shall/Should/Can** I get you some more coffee?
❼ **Shall/Should** I call you next week?

Remember

Informell bittet man um Erlaubnis mit can ❶. Um zu fragen, ob etwas offiziell erlaubt ist, benutzt man oft be allowed to ❷. Diese Form wird auch für *future*, *present* und *past perfect* sowie mit anderen modalen Hilfsverben verwendet ❸. Eine etwas höflichere Bitte stellt man mit **may** or **could** ❹ ❺.

Shall I and Should I, oder sehr informell Can I, werden oft benutzt, um Hilfe anzubieten ❻, können aber auch verwendet werden, um zu fragen, wie man bei einer bestimmten Gelegenheit vorgehen sollte ❼.

2 Ashley ist jetzt bei ihrem dritten Vorstellungsgespräch.

Vervollständigen Sie die Sätze mit der richtigen Form von can, may, be allowed to, shall oder should. Schreiben Sie dann, wer dies Ihrer Meinung nach gesagt hat – Ashley (A) oder das Firmenpersonal (F).

1. ________ I sit here? ____
2. ________ I get you another cup of coffee? ____
3. Miss, you're not ________ park there! ____
4. ________ I give you my mobile number? ____
5. ________ I send you another reference (= Arbeitszeugnis)? ____
6. *(To a friend by mobile)* Tom, help! ________ you give me Dr Smith's telephone number? ____
7. Sorry, you ________ use that photocopier. It's only for employees. ____
8. ________ I call you at home? ____
9. ________ I contact you if I don't hear anything? ____
10. ________ I fill in all of these forms? ____
11. Will I ________ use the company car if I get the job? ____
12. You ________ call me if you have any questions about the job. ____
13. ________ I send the CV by email or regular post? ____
14. I think you ________ give my data to any other firm. ____
15. *(To a friend)* Tom, it's me again! ________ you meet me at the Red Lion Pub in 20 minutes. I'm exhausted. ____

5.3 Notwendigkeit: *must, have (got) to, needn't* Ratschlag/Aufforderung: *ought to, should, had better, be (supposed) to*

Read the examples

1. All employees **must** wear safety glasses when operating this machine.
2. Employees **mustn't** use the lift in case of fire.
3. The appointment is at 9 a.m. and I **have (got) to** be on time!
4. I **needn't** take my CV. They already have it.
5. You **ought to/should** wear something a bit more conservative.
6. I **had better** learn something about the firm. They are sure to ask me.
7. I **am (supposed) to** go to Room 530 for my interview.

Remember

Must (müssen) wird nur für die Gegenwart verwendet. Es betont, dass der Sprecher Autorität hat, etwas anzuordnen bzw. zu verbieten (**mustn't**) ❶ ❷.
Beachten Sie: Die Übersetzung von mustn't ist **nicht** „nicht müssen", sondern „nicht dürfen".

Im Alltagsgespräch wird ansonsten **have to** bevorzugt verwendet, um eine Notwendigkeit auszudrücken. **Have got to** betont etwas die Dringlichkeit, wird allerdings nur in der Gegenwart benutzt ❸.

Needn't, don't have to und **haven't got to** stehen alle gleichbedeutend für „nicht müssen" ❹.

Be to, be supposed to, had better, ought to und **should** entsprechen dem deutschen „sollen" und drücken unterschiedliche Grade von Dringlichkeit aus:
Be to verwendet man für klare Anweisungen oder Aufforderungen. Es ist eine Art höfliches „müssen". **Be supposed to** verwendet man für Mitteilungen, Anweisungen, Aufforderungen oder Ratschläge, wenn diese Aussagen von anderen Personen stammen ❼.
Ought to und **should** dienen dem Ausdruck von allgemeinen Aufforderungen und Ratschlägen ❺. In verneinten Sätzen steht immer **shouldn't**.
Had better kann einen dringend gemeinten Ratschlag ausdrücken, der einer Warnung nahekommt ❻.

3 Ergänzen Sie die Sätze mit einer passenden englischen Übersetzung des deutschen modalen Hilfsverbs. Es gibt manchmal mehrere Möglichkeiten.

1. You (müssen) ____________ to work eight hours a day, but you (nicht müssen) ____________ start at 8.
2. You (nicht dürfen) ____________ come later than 10 however. That's a company rule!
3. You (sollen) ____________ take a Spanish course sometime.
4. Just a warning from me. You (nicht sollen) ____________ tell anything private to that colleague over there. She'll tell everyone else in the office.
5. Look at this memo from the office manager. All of the employees (sollen) ____________ dress in a way that is suitable for a business situation.

6. There are a lot of other employees here who would like a promotion (= Beförderung) so I (sollen) ______ do that job really well.

4 Ordnen Sie diese Sätze den richtigen Überbegriffen zu.

I ought to do it. *I've got to do it.* *I needn't do it.* *I must do it.* *I'm supposed to do it.* *I haven't got to do it.* *I mustn't do it.* *I am to do it.* *I don't have to do it.* *I had better do it.* *I should do it.* *I have to do it.*

Necessary	Strongly advisable	Advisable	Not necessary

5 Übersetzen Sie die folgenden Sätze ins Englische.

1. Wir müssen keine Uniformen tragen.

2. Wir müssen uns aber geschäftsmäßig anziehen.

3. Wir dürfen keine Shorts oder engen Röcke tragen.

4. Sie sollten nicht wieder zu spät kommen, Sie könnten Ihren Job verlieren.

5. Wir sollen noch drei Bewerber interviewen, doch ich weiß jetzt, wen ich einstellen muss.

6. Der Chef sagt, dass ich nächste Woche in einer anderen Abteilung arbeiten soll.

5.4 Annahme/Wahrscheinlichkeit: *must, may, might, could, is said to, is supposed to, is considered to*

Read the examples

Look at the man over there with the CEO.

❶ He **must** be our new boss. (He **has (got) to** be our new boss.)
❷ He **can't** be the new secretary.
❸ He **might/may/could** be younger than our new boss, but it's hard to tell.
❹ He **is said to** know/**is supposed to** know a lot about the Asian market.
❺ He **is considered to** be (**is supposed to** be/**is said to** be) an expert on Asia.

Remember

Wenn wir betonen wollen, dass wir ziemlich sicher in einer Annahme sind, benutzen wir must mit der Grundform eines Verbs ❶. Seltener wird dieselbe Sicherheit mit have (got) to ausgedrückt.
Beachten Sie: Auch hier ist mustn't nicht das Gegenteil von must.

Für Annahmen, dass etwas mit Sicherheit nicht der Fall ist, benutzt man **can't** ❷.

Wenn über die (weniger sichere) Wahrscheinlichkeit einer Situation spekuliert wird, benutzt man might/may/could als modale Hilfsverben mit gleicher Bedeutung ❸.

Mit einer Passivkonstruktion des Verbs + Infinitiv drückt man Spekulationen aus
▷ über etwas, das gesagt wird (is said to),
▷ über etwas, das vermutet wird (is supposed to), oder
▷ über etwas, das man meint (is thought to/is considered to) ❹ ❺.

6 **Ordnen Sie jeder der Situationen 1–10 eine passende Erklärung a–j zu und ergänzen Sie diese mit einem passenden modalen Hilfsverb aus der Liste unten. Auch wenn es mehrere Möglichkeiten gibt, benutzen Sie jedes modale Hilfsverb höchstens zweimal.**

must *can't* *may* *might* *could*

1. The letter isn't on my desk.
2. The photocopier isn't working.
3. I've never seen the woman at that desk before.
4. The espresso machine isn't in the kitchen.
5. Those clouds look rather dark and threatening.
6. Our boss is looking at office equipment catalogues.

7. I'm sure that clock over there is wrong.
8. Business has been really good for the firm this year.
9. Do you think there are too many people in the lift?
10. Nobody answers the phone, and I know they're in the office today.

a It ______ be 5.30. My watch says 4 o'clock and I know it's right.

b He ______ want to get new desks. That would be great. We really need them.

c It ______ be out of paper, but I'm not sure.

d I ______ have the wrong number.

e They ______ have it in the conference room. There's a meeting there and they always serve espresso.

f If we're lucky, we ______ get a bonus.

g It ______ be in the post already. I haven't got another explanation.

h She ______ be the new employee they told us about, but I don't really know.

i Perhaps there are. It ______ set off the alarm.

j It ______ start raining, but you never know about the weather.

7 Übersetzen Sie die folgenden Sätze. Benutzen Sie dazu das angegebene Verb.

1. Diese Drucker sollen die besten auf dem Markt sein. (say)

   These printers ______.

2. Sie sollen auch sehr wenig kosten. (suppose)

   They ______.

3. Warum ist John hier? Er sollte in Hamburg sein. (suppose)

   Why is John here? He ______.

4. Ergonomische Hocker sollen besser für den Rücken sein. (consider)

   Ergonomic stools ______.

5. Die Kriminalität soll eines der größten Probleme in dieser Gegend sein. (think)

   Crime ______.

6. Maria soll viele Sprachen kennen. (say)

   Maria ______________________________.

7. Diese Kantine soll sehr gutes Essen haben. (say)

   This canteen ______________________________.

8. Yoga soll gut für die Konzentration sein. (consider)

   Yoga ______________________________.

Vergangenheit und Zukunft

Read the examples

❶ That man with the CEO yesterday **can't have been** the new boss. He was much too young.
❷ He was a student. He **must have been looking** for an internship.
❸ Where's my wallet? I **must have left** it in the car.
❹ She was really early, but there **might not have been** much traffic on the M4.
❺ He **is said to have been** a great football player when he was younger.
❻ Several of our colleagues **might be going** to the trade fair in Bristol next week.
❼ Ashley **is supposed to be visiting** our branch in Hove next month.

Remember

Um Vermutungen über **vergangene Situationen** anzustellen, benutzt man immer die modalen Hilfsverben zusammen mit dem *present perfect simple* ❶ ❸ ❹ ❺ oder *progressive* ❷.
Beachten Sie: Zusammen mit modalen Hilfsverben werden nie Verben im *simple past* benutzt, auch nicht in Sätzen mit bestimmten Zeitangaben.

Will man verdeutlichen, dass es sich um Vermutungen über **Geschehnisse in der Zukunft** handelt, benutzt man modale Hilfsverben + be + Verb in der *-ing*-Form ❻ ❼.
Beachten Sie: In verneinten Sätzen benutzt man **nicht** could.

8 **Benutzen Sie ein passendes modales Hilfsverb mit einem Verb in der richtigen Zeit, um die Schlussfolgerung anders auszudrücken.**

1. Look at all the rubbish in the conference room. I'm sure someone has had a party here recently.

   Someone must ______ a party here.

2. I'm sure they didn't try to clean it up afterwards.

   They can't ______ to clean it up.

3. There are so many trees and branches lying around the parking lot. I'm sure there was a big storm here.

   There ______ a big storm here last night.

4. John isn't at his desk. Perhaps he went on holiday.

   John ______ on holiday.

5. There was so much noise upstairs this morning. Perhaps the colleagues upstairs were moving the furniture around.

   They ______ the furniture around.

6. John's suitcase is next to his desk. Perhaps he'll go on his business trip straight from work.

   John ______ on his business trip straight from work.

7. I wonder why Tim called the travel agent. Perhaps he's going to fly to Milan.

   Tim ______.

8. People say that Garcia is an excellent programmer.

   Garcia ______.

9. The weather is so terrible. Perhaps we won't drive to the conference next weekend after all.

   We ______.

10. Did you hear about his secretary? Many people say that she is going to get married next week.

    She ______.

5.5 Frühere Gewohnheit/Zustand: *used to be*
„an etwas gewöhnt sein": *be used to* + *-ing*-Form

Read the examples

❶ Tom **used to have** a simple job in an American supermarket, but today he's an office clerk.
❷ **Did** he **use to work** different shifts (= Schichten)?
❸ Yes, but now he **is used to working** from 9 to 5 every day.
❹ And he had to **get used to wearing** a suit to work every day.

Remember

Used to gibt es nur in der Vergangenheitsform, es beschreibt frühere Gewohnheiten und Zustände. Es entspricht dem deutschen „pflegte zu tun" oder „früher" + Verb ❶❷.

Beachten Sie: Es gibt etwas ähnliche Konstruktionen mit völlig anderer Bedeutung.
Be used to doing something bedeutet „an etwas gewöhnt sein" ❸.
Get used to doing something bedeutet „sich an etwas gewöhnen" ❹.

9 Tom, ein Kollege Ashleys im Büro, arbeitete einige Jahren in einem amerikanischen Supermarkt, bevor er seine Stelle als Bürokaufmann in ihrer Firma bekam.

Entscheiden Sie, welche der folgenden Sätze zu seinem früheren Supermarkt-Job passen, und ergänzen Sie mit used to. Die anderen Sätze ergänzen Sie mit didn't use to.

1. Tom ______ work at the check-out counter (= Kasse).
2. Tom ______ sit at a desk all day.
3. Tom ______ wear a suit and tie to work.
4. Tom ______ work the night shift quite often.
5. Tom ______ sort out the bad fruit and vegetables.
6. Tom ______ count the money in the cash register every evening.
7. Tom ______ write a lot of emails and letters to customers.
8. Tom ______ check and stock the food on the shelves.

9. Tom ________ have his own desk and computer for work.
10. Tom ________ earn as much money as now.

10 Tom muss sich in seinem neuen Job an einige Dinge gewöhnen, an andere Dinge nicht.

Bilden Sie englische Sätze.

Er war es nicht gewohnt, ...

1. ... so viel zu sitzen.

   He ________.

2. ... häufig am Telefon zu sein.

   ________.

3. ... nie tagsüber frei zu haben.

   ________.

Er war es gewohnt, ...

4. ... Kundenbeschwerden zu hören.

   ________ *customers' complaints.*

5. ... wenig Zeit für eine Mittagspause zu haben.

   ________.

6. ... zu Fuß zur Arbeit zu gehen.

   ________.

Er musste sich an Folgendes gewöhnen:

7. ... mit der Bahn zur Arbeit zu fahren.

   ________.

8. ... viel Englisch mit Kunden zu reden.

   ________.

9. ... viele Stunden pro Tag am Computer zu verbringen.

   ________.

6 DAS VERB „LASSEN“

Thema: An endangered planet

6.1 Zulassen

Read the examples

❶ China doesn't want to **let** its population **grow** too fast.
❷ The state **allows/permits** each family **to have** one child.

Remember

let allow permit	somebody	do **to** do **to** do	something

„Jemanden etwas machen lassen“ im Sinne von „etwas zulassen/erlauben“ wird im Englischen entweder mit let somebody do something oder mit allow/permit somebody to do something ausgedrückt ❶ ❷. Im alltäglichen Gebrauch wird let bevorzugt.

1 Unsere Erde ist ein gefährdeter Planet – gefährdet unter anderem durch eine Bevölkerungsexplosion. Bei einer Konferenz in New York äußern sich verschiedene Experten zu diesem Thema.

Verwenden Sie die Wörter in Klammern, um die Sätze mit let oder allow/permit ... to zu vervollständigen. Achten Sie dabei auf die Wortstellung.

1. We must *let people have* (people/have/let) free information on birth control (= Geburtenkontrolle).
2. We should ______ (everyone/allow/obtain) condoms free of charge (= kostenlos) in the battle against AIDS.
3. It's important ______ (not let/become/big cities) even bigger – like Tokyo with 20 million!
4. In China we ______ (women/not permit/marry) before the age of 25.
5. Egypt must ______ (not let/increase/its population) by more than 2% a year.

6.2 Machen lassen

Read the examples

❶ Last year the town **had/got** 50,000 tons of glass **recycled** by our company.
❷ **Did** the company **have/get** those chemicals **removed**?

Remember

„Etwas machen lassen“ wird im Englischen mit einer Form von have/get + Objekt + Partizip Perfekt wiedergegeben ❶ ❷. Eigentlich ist get mit have austauschbar. Obwohl get als umgangssprachlich gilt, taucht es in allen Bereichen immer häufiger auf.

Beachten Sie:
He **had it repaired.** = Er ließ es reparieren.
He **had repaired it.** = Er hatte es repariert.

2 Der Bürgermeister von Harrisburg im US-Bundesstaat Pennsylvania versucht seit längerer Zeit, der Müllprobleme der Stadt Herr zu werden. Bei einer Bürgerversammlung bemängelt er, dass nicht genug getan worden ist.

Vervollständigen Sie die folgenden Sätze durch die Wörter in Klammern. Verwenden Sie jeweils (not) have + Objekt und Partizip – manchmal muss nicht der Infinitiv, sondern eine andere Form von have eingesetzt werden. Achten Sie auf die Wortstellung.

1. Six months ago this city *had a plan drawn up* (a plan/draw up = entwerfen) for a garbage incinerator (= Müllverbrennungsanlage). Well, we *haven't had it* ______ (not/it/build) yet, but work will start soon.
2. Let me tell you that the city council intends to ______ (improvements/introduce) in the collection of garbage. We want to ______ (things/organize) much more efficiently from now on.
3. I wanted to ______ (new containers/design) for used batteries, but we need more money for it.

4. But we must ______________ (these containers/produce) if we are going to solve the problem.
5. Last year we ______________ (not/a recycling plant/construct) as planned – money was again the problem.
6. I hope that next year the city ______________ (the river/clean up). It's full of toxic (= giftig) waste from the steel company. I intend to ______________ (them/sue = verklagen) if they don't do anything about it!

6.3 Veranlassen

Read the examples

❶ I think they should **have** every government in the EU **stop** the production of electricity from nuclear power.
Yes, they should **get** them **to stop** it immediately.
❷ I'm sure new laws will **make** the nuclear industry **change** its attitude.
Well, sometimes it **makes** me **scream** to see how little has changed so far.
❸ The nuclear power plant (= Atomkraftwerk) **was made to close**.

Remember

„Jemanden **veranlassen**, etwas zu tun“ wird im Englischen mit have someone do something oder mit get somebody **to** do something wiedergegeben ❶. Have und get sind austauschbar, get wird jedoch vor allem in der Umgangssprache bevorzugt.

To make somebody do something bedeutet zwar auch „veranlassen“, jedoch mehr im Sinne von „jemanden dazu **zwingen/bringen**, etwas zu tun“ ❷. Im Passiv wird make mit to + Infinitiv verwendet ❸.

get have make	somebody	**to** do do do	something
be made **to** do			

Im Deutschen werden diese Formen sehr häufig durch **zwingen** bzw. **(veran)lassen** wiedergegeben.

3 Eine eindeutige Gefahr liegt für unseren Planeten in der Zerstörung der Ozonschicht (= ozone layer) durch FCKW (= CFC), das u. a. als Treibgas (= propellant) in Sprühdosen verwendet wird. Was bedeutet dies für die Menschen sowie für die Erderwärmung? Hier sind einige Kommentare dazu aus dem US-Nachrichtenmagazin *Epoch*.

Verwenden Sie die Wörter in Klammern, um untenstehende Sätze durch die folgenden Strukturen (oder eine entsprechende Form davon) zu vervollständigen. Achten Sie dabei auf die Wortstellung.

(not) have + Objekt + Infinitiv

(not) make + Objekt + Infinitiv

Subjekt + (not) be made to

1. It's time to *have industrial nations end* (end/industrial nations/have) CFC production everywhere.
2. The chemical industry in many parts of the world *hasn't been made* ______ (not be made/do) this so far.
3. Chlorine (= Chlor) atoms in CFCs destroy ozone, and it's important to ______ (make/understand/the public) that this is a danger to health – and they must ______ (realize/be made) that the problem is global.
4. The ozone layer over Greenland, the Arctic and the Antarctic is getting thinner – if the ice ______ (melt/be made) too fast, the sea level (= Meeresspiegel) will rise.
5. A thinner ozone layer is certain to ______ (skin cancer/make/increase).
6. If the industrial nations ______ (not be made/take) action, many islands in the Pacific will disappear under water!
7. To help the environment, we should ______ (develop/have/scientists) efficient fuel cells (= Brennstoffzellen) for cars and ______ (them/do/not have) research (= Forschung) into biological weapons.

8. We ought to ______ (every state/have/sign) the Kyoto Protocol and any follow-up agreements. It's enough to ______ (cry/make/you) when you see what's happening to our planet.

4 Wie soll man die heutigen Umweltprobleme bekämpfen? Hier sind einige Beschlüsse einer ökologischen Gruppe.

Vervollständigen Sie die Sätze mit get und dem Verb in Klammern. (Und to nicht vergessen!)

1. *Get* every country on earth *to cease* (cease = aufhören) making CFCs now!
2. ______ the USA and the EU ______ (close) their nuclear plants!
3. ______ our politicians ______ (ban = verbieten) nuclear power!
4. ______ the public ______ (protest) against globalisation!

7 DAS GERUNDIUM UND DER INFINITIV

Thema: Ernest Hemingway

7.1 Gerundium nach Verben und Wendungen

Read the examples

❶ Most authors can't **imagine winning** the Nobel Prize.
❷ It's **no use complaining** if you don't win it, but it's the one literature prize it's certainly **worth receiving**.

Remember

Das Gerundium steht als Objekt nach bestimmten **Verben** wie: admit, avoid, carry on, consider, deny, detest (verabscheuen), dislike, endure (ertragen), enjoy, finish, give up, hate, can't help (nicht umhinkönnen), include, imagine, keep (on) (etwas weiterhin tun), like, love, mind, miss, quit (aufhören), practise, prefer, resent (übel nehmen), resist (widerstehen), stand (aushalten), start, stop, suggest ❶.

Das Gerundium steht außerdem nach bestimmten **Ausdrücken** wie:
it's (no) fun, it's no good, it's no use, there's no point/sense (in), there's no (denying), to be busy, to feel like, to be worth ❷.

1 Hier sind Auszüge aus einer Biografie über den großen amerikanischen Schriftsteller Ernest Hemingway (1899–1961).

Vervollständigen Sie diese Sätze mit dem Gerundium.

1. Hemingway grew up in Oak Park, a Chicago suburb. Like most kids he didn't particularly enjoy *attending* (attend) school. He preferred ______ (fish) and ______ (play) football instead.
2. As a child he hated ______ (be told) what to do and loved ______ (show) his parents, especially his mother, how independent he was.
3. In childhood and in later years Hemingway resented ______ (not get) what he wanted and always disliked people ______ (not let) him have his own way (= sich durchsetzen).
4. Ernest and his father, a prominent doctor, both loved ______

(hunt). With his father as his teacher the boy practised ______ (shoot) from the very early age of twelve.

5. In fact, Ernest never gave up ______ (catch) fish and ______ (slaughter = niedermetzeln) wild animals to the very end of his life. Even his best friends spoke of his "killer instinct", but nobody suggested ______ (attempt = versuchen) to change him.
6. To see animals die was something that he never denied ______ (find) great satisfaction in.
7. In 1917, America entered the First World War. Hemingway considered ______ (join) the army and ______ (help) his country, but was sent to Italy with the Red Cross instead.
8. It seems that for most of his life he couldn't help ______ (become) involved in wars and adventures all over the world.
9. Above all, he could never quit ______ (try) to show that he was braver than everyone else.

2 Übersetzen Sie die Satzteile in Klammern jeweils mit dem Gerundium und einem entsprechenden Ausdruck.

1. *There's no sense (in)/point (in) looking for* (Es hat keinen Zweck, ... zu suchen) a meaning to life in Hemingway's novels; his motto was: "______." (Es ist sinnlos zu leben.)
2. He never slept late and, particularly in the mornings, he was always ______ on one of his books. (damit beschäftigt, ... zu arbeiten)
3. In the afternoons he usually ______ something active, such as fishing. (hatte Lust, ... zu tun)
4. ______ for him ______ at home. (Es machte keinen Spaß, ... zu sitzen)
5. ______ that he was a heavy drinker. (Es lässt sich nicht bestreiten, ...)

7.2 Infinitiv anstatt Gerundium

Read the examples

1. A lot of script writers (= Drehbuchautor) **decide to live** in Hollywood.
2. The paparazi will **start taking/to take** photos as soon as she arrives.

Remember

Nach einigen gängigen Verben verwendet man anstelle des Gerundiums den Infinitiv. Wie beim Gerundium muss man diese Verben auswendig lernen. Die wichtigsten sind:
afford, agree, appear, attempt, choose, dare (wagen), decide, expect, fail (unterlassen; es nicht schaffen/fertigbringen), help, hope, learn, manage (schaffen), offer, plan, promise, refuse, seem, wish ➊.

Nach begin, continue, intend, start kann entweder ein Gerundium oder ein Infinitiv stehen. Die Bedeutung bleibt gleich ➋.

3 **Vervollständigen Sie diesen Text über den jungen Ernest Hemingway, indem Sie ein Gerundium oder einen Infinitiv einsetzen.**

After he had left high school – where he had already begun *to write/writing* [1] (write) articles for the school newspaper, *The Trapeze* – Hemingway chose ________ [2] (work) for the *Kansas City Star.* He hoped ________ [3] (learn) as much as possible there about journalism. It was a time in his life he appears ________ [4] (have enjoyed), and he certainly did not seem ________ [5] (miss) ________ [6] (not have to) live at home anymore with his parents. He hated his mother, and critics would love ________ [7] (know) exactly why; others would love ________ [8] (find out) the real reasons for his father's suicide.
In 1918, Hemingway intended ________ [9] (go) to France as a soldier, but he failed ________ [10] (pass) the medical test and so went to Italy as

an ambulance driver. In Italy he managed ________ [11] (get sent) to the front, though he risked ________ [12] (be killed). In fact, he was seriously wounded and expected ________ [13] (die). For at least six months he avoided ________ [14] (sleep) in the dark – the light was always on. He admitted ________ [15] (feel) afraid of death. After the war he returned to Chicago, but felt he would prefer ________ [16] (not stay) there. He wished ________ [17] (become) a writer and so went to Paris. Another writer, Sherwood Anderson, had suggested Hemingway's ________ [18] (move) there and offered ________ [19] (introduce) him to the Paris literary world.

7.3 Bedeutungsunterschiede

Read the examples

1	I can't **remember/forget meeting** him.	sich erinnern/vergessen, etwas getan zu haben
2	I **remembered/forgot to write down** the ISBN of that book.	daran denken/vergessen, etwas zu tun
3	**Stop talking!**	aufhören, etwas zu tun
4	We **stopped to look around** the new bookshop.	anhalten, um etwas (anderes) zu tun
5	You can't **go on eating** during the lesson!	etwas weiterhin tun
6	Let's leave that theme and **go on to discuss** your new film.	etwas anderes als Nächstes tun
7	I've **tried to understand** Shakespeare in the original, but it's too hard. Then **try using** a translation instead.	sich bemühen, etwas zu tun etwas (aus)probieren

Remember

Die Verben forget, go on, remember, stop, try haben völlig unterschiedliche Bedeutungen, je nachdem, ob ein Gerundium oder ein Infinitiv darauf folgt ❶ - ❼.

4 Übersetzen Sie die fehlenden Satzteile. Verwenden Sie dabei die folgenden Verben mit Gerundium oder Infinitiv.

~~forget (2 x)~~ go on (2 x) remember (2 x) stop (2 x)

1. Sie wird nie vergessen, wie sie Hemingway zum ersten Mal las.

   She'll never forget ______ Hemingway for the first time.

2. Vergiss nicht, mir das Buch zu besorgen.

   ______ *forget* ______ me the book.

3. Denken Sie bitte daran, den nächsten Text sorgfältiger zu analysieren (analyse).

   ______ the next text more carefully.

4. Sie konnte sich nicht erinnern, dass sie Hemingways Haus in Key West besucht hatte.

   ______ Hemingway's house in Key West.

5. Bei einer Reise hat sie haltgemacht, um sein Haus zu besichtigen (look around).

   ______ his house on a trip.

6. Sein Leben lang konnte Hemingway nicht aufhören, seine Mutter zu hassen.

   ______ his mother his whole life long.

7. Trotz vieler Warnungen trank er weiter.

   ______ despite lots of warnings.

8. Nach der Einleitung besprach sie als Nächstes ihre Gedichte.

   ______ her poems after the introduction.

7.4 Gerundium nach Präpositionen

Read the examples

❶ Hemingway was very **keen on** (= begeistert von) **boxing**.
❷ He **dreamed of becoming** greater than Shakespeare and felt nothing would **prevent** him **from doing** so.
❸ The authors of this book have no **hope of being** famous.

Remember

Verben, die auf eine Präposition (außer to) folgen, stehen im Gerundium.

Die Präposition kann verbunden sein mit einem

▷ **Adjektiv**: accustomed to (daran gewöhnt, etwas zu tun), afraid of, angry about/at, bad at, crazy about, disappointed about/at, excited about, fed up with, fond of (etwas gerne tun oder haben), good at, happy about/at, interested in, keen on, proud of, sick of, tired of, used to (daran gewöhnt, etwas zu tun), worried about ❶,
▷ **Verb**: apologize for, believe in, congratulate somebody on (gratulieren), concentrate on, consist of, cope with, decide against, depend on, dream of, insist on, prevent somebody from, succeed in, stop somebody from, specialize in, suspect somebody of (verdächtigen), thank somebody for, warn somebody against ❷,
▷ **Substantiv**: advantage of, chance of, danger of, difficulty in, hope of, method of, possibility of, reason for, trouble in ❸.

5 Ernest Hemingway führte ein recht abenteuerliches und bewegtes Leben – als Kriegskorrespondent, als Großwildjäger und auch in der Ehe.

Vervollständigen Sie diese Sätze über ihn mit Präposition und Gerundium.

1. He was afraid *of* people *seeing* (see) that he was extremely sensitive.
2. He was proud ______ (be able to) box extremely well and wouldn't dream ______ (not fight) even very good boxers. He certainly wasn't used ______ (have) anybody beat him.
3. After World War I he decided ______ (live) in Oak Park. He was interested ______ (learn) how to write, but saw no possibility ______ (do) that in the States.

4. At that time Paris was the centre of the literary world, and Hemingway believed that there he could concentrate __________ (write) the way he wanted to. He went to Paris in 1921.
5. From 1939 Hemingway lived in Cuba. He had bought a large boat which he insisted __________ (use) in World War II to hunt for German submarines near Cuba. Nobody could prevent him __________ (risk) his life in this way.
6. By 1943 he had grown fed up __________ (spend) his time in Cuba and so he became a correspondent. By 1944 he had succeeded __________ (get transferred = sich versetzen lassen) to Normandy.
7. Although his job consisted __________ (report) and not much else, he had difficulty __________ (accept) that he was a correspondent and not a soldier. He was disappointed __________ (do) the work of a journalist.
8. Hemingway was married four times and seems to have had trouble __________ (cope with) his wives – particularly number three, Martha Gellhorn, who was also a well-known writer and accustomed __________ (behave) independently. Hemingway, the macho, hated independent women!
9. By the end of his life Hemingway had become senile. He suspected the FBI __________ (want) to put him in prison. He shot himself in 1961.
10. Hemingway had a special style of writing. He avoided abstract nouns and concentrated __________ (put) as many concrete nouns as possible in his work; in his dialogue he specialized __________ (form) very short sentences and was never keen __________ (add) lots of facts. This was his way __________ (describe) 'reality'.

8 DAS PARTIZIP

Thema: Wild animals and poachers

8.1 Adverbialsätze

Read the examples

1. He grew tired **(while) waiting** for the jeep to arrive.
   (... while he was waiting ...)
2. **After reaching/Having reached** the game reserve (= Wildreservat), the tourists started to take photos.
   (After the tourists had reached ..., they ...)
3. The zebra **being** injured, the lion killed it easily.
   (As/Because/Since the zebra was injured, the lion ...)
4. **If shot** in such large numbers, they'll disappear completely.
   (If they are shot ...)

Remember

Um den Adverbialsatz verkürzen zu können, braucht man das **gleiche Subjekt** im Haupt- und Nebensatz ①. Solche Nebensätze verwendet man häufig in der Schriftsprache.

Ist das Subjekt des Adverbialsatzes ein **Substantiv**, so rückt es bei der Verkürzung in den **Hauptsatz** ②.

Bei kausalen Nebensätzen (as, because, since) ist eine Verkürzung auch bei **zwei verschiedenen Subjekten** möglich ③. Bei einer solchen Verkürzung entfällt as, because oder since. Das Partizip Perfekt steht häufig nach (al)though, if, unless, until, when ④.

1 Mashatu ist ein Wildreservat in Botswana, einem Staat im südlichen Afrika. Gareth Patterson hat dort einige Jahre als Wildhüter (= game warden) gearbeitet. Gareth war vor allem bemüht, die letzten Löwen in Mashatu zu schützen. In einem Interview für eine Londoner Zeitung sprach er über seine Arbeit.

Ersetzen Sie jeden Adverbialsatz durch ein Partizip Präsens oder ein Partizip Perfekt. (Manchmal muss das Subjekt in den Hauptsatz rücken!)

1. Before I was able to write my book, I had to study lions in the wild.

   Before being able to write my book, I had to study lions in the wild.

2. Although lions are disappearing fast, they still live in large numbers in East Africa.

   Although ______ fast, *lions* still live in large numbers in East Africa.

3. Because I love these animals the way I do, I decided to learn more about them.

   ______ these animals the way I do, I decided to learn more about them.

4. As they aren't especially timid (= scheu), lions are fairly easy to photograph.

   ______ especially timid, lions are fairly easy to photograph.

5. After I'd watched and counted the lions in Mashatu, I gave some of them names.

   ______ and ______ the lions in Mashatu, I gave some of them names.

6. When a lion is caught by poachers (= Wilderer), it's often sold to a zoo in Europe or the USA.

   ______ by poachers, ______ is often sold to a zoo in Europe or the USA.

7. Unless the poachers are stopped soon, they'll destroy everything.

   ______ soon, ______ will destroy everything.

8. If we're given more help against them, perhaps we can save some of the animals.

   ______ more help against them, perhaps we can save some of the animals.

9. I was once attacked while I was trying to destroy some poachers' traps (= Falle).

   I was once attacked ______ to destroy some poachers' traps.

10. Since I had to fight three of them, they won easily.

    ______ fight three of them, they won easily.

11. After I had been attacked once, I never went anywhere without my rifle again.

    ______ once, I never went anywhere without my rifle again.

12. When a lion skin (= Fell) is sold in Europe or America, it makes a big profit.

    ______ in Europe or America, ______ makes a big profit.

8.2 Verschiedene Nebensätze

Read the examples

❶ Chris fell over, **hurting** his head.
(..., wobei er ...)
❷ "Might be a hippo," Jim said, **picking up** his camera.
(..., indem ...)
❸ Jim waited all day, **hoping** to see a rhino.
(... und hoffte ...)
❹ **With** the dry season (= Trockenzeit) **having started**, it won't rain again.
(Jetzt wo ...)

Remember

Das Partizip Präsens kann einen Teilsatz ersetzen, der im Deutschen durch „wobei", „indem", „und (dabei)" eingeleitet wird. Eine Verkürzung ist möglich, da es nur **ein Subjekt** gibt ❶ ❷ ❸.

Das Partizip nach with wird sowohl formell als auch umgangssprachlich viel verwendet, vor allem, wenn Haupt- und Nebensatz **verschiedene Subjekte** haben. Im Deutschen wird diese Konstruktion oft mit „da", „heutzutage/jetzt wo", „seit(dem)", „weil", „wenn" übersetzt ❹.

2 Weil sowohl in Zoos als auch bei Privatleuten eine große Nachfrage nach ihnen besteht, sind einige Tierarten in Afrika von der Ausrottung bedroht.

Aus zwei Sätzen bilden Sie jeweils einen Satz mit dem Partizip Präsens. (Und denken Sie auch an das Komma!)

1. Poachers kill lots of lions. They receive very little, however, for a skin.

   Poachers kill lots of lions, *receiving* very little, however, for a skin.

2. They stay very poor. They hope to earn at least enough for their family.

   They stay very poor, ________ to earn at least enough for their family.

3. Traders (= Händler) in animal skins buy from the poachers. They make a good profit out of it.

   Traders in animal skins buy from the poachers, ________ a good profit out of it.

4. An animal may stay in a trap for days. It dies of thirst fairly soon.
   An animal may stay in a trap for days, ______ of thirst fairly soon.
5. One of Gareth Patterson's favourite lions got caught. She freed herself only after she'd bitten off her paw (= Pfote).
   One of Gareth Patterson's favourite lions got caught, ______ herself only after she'd bitten off her paw.
6. The poachers have all sorts of weapons. They use machine guns (= Maschinengewehr), for example, to kill elephants.
   The poachers have all sorts of weapons, ______ machine guns, for example, to kill elephants.
7. Ivory (= Elfenbein) is very valuable. It's sold in Europe and Asia at high prices.
   Ivory is very valuable, ______ in Europe and Asia at high prices.
8. The Chinese use ivory in certain medicines. They pay a great deal to obtain it.
   The Chinese use ivory in certain medicines, ______ a great deal to obtain it.
9. The Government of Botswana tries hard to protect the animals. It aims (= beabsichtigen) to attract tourists to the country.
   The Government of Botswana tries hard to protect the animals, ______ to attract tourists to the country.

3 Vervollständigen Sie die folgenden Sätze, indem Sie die Wörter in Klammern durch ein Partizip Präsens mit with übersetzen.

1. (Da Elfenbein so teuer ist) *With ivory being so expensive*, the traders are making a lot of money.
2. (Seitdem die Anzahl der Wilderer steigt) ______, many governments in Africa are alarmed.
3. How can the lions of Mashatu survive (wenn so viele Leute sie jagen) ______?

4. (Weil die Elefanten immer schneller verschwinden) ____________________ , they'll all be gone by the year 2040.

5. (Da so viele geschossen werden) ____________________ , the numbers are falling daily.

6. (Da die Situation so schlimm geworden ist) ____________________ , we must act immediately.

8.3 Relativsätze und Wendungen

Read the examples

1. The man **holding** the rifle is a trader.
   (The man that/who is holding ...) → Verlaufsform
2. He bought it from the hunters **standing** over there.
   (... the hunters that/who are standing ...) → Verlaufsform
3. The hunt **arranged** for Saturday will be cancelled.
   (The hunt that/which has been arranged ...)
4. **Strictly speaking**, nobody can stop the poachers.
   (Genau genommen ...)

Remember

Durch holding, standing und arranged ist der Relativsatz verkürzt worden, was im Grunde nur mit einem notwendigen Relativsatz möglich ist und nur dann, wenn das Relativpronomen **Subjekt** des Relativsatzes ist ❶ ❷ ❸.
Die Verkürzung durch *-ing* (Partizip Präsens mit aktiver Bedeutung) drückt aus, dass jemand gerade etwas tut. Diese Form ist möglich, wenn in dem unverkürzten Satz eine **Verlaufsform** verwendet werden muss ❶ ❷.

Das **Partizip Perfekt** hat passive Bedeutung ❸.

Es gibt eine Reihe von idiomatischen Wendungen mit Partizip ❹. Sie kommen recht häufig im Alltagsgebrauch vor: considering (that) (wenn man bedenkt, ...), generally/roughly/strictly speaking, health/time/weather permitting, judging from (nach ... zu urteilen), speaking/talking of (da gerade von ... die Rede ist), supposing (that) (angenommen), provide/providing (that) (vorausgesetzt).

4 Ersetzen Sie jeweils den Relativsatz in Klammern durch ein Partizip Präsens oder ein Partizip Perfekt.

1. Two of the poachers (that were arrested) *arrested* yesterday will have to go to prison.
2. The symbol (which has been used) ______ by the World Wildlife Fund since 1961 is that of the panda.
3. Recently in China, a man (who had been accused) ______ of killing a panda was hanged.
4. The real problem is the rich consumers (that are destroying) ______ the world's wildlife indirectly with their greed (= Gier).
5. The problems (that have been occurring) ______ in Mashatu and (which have been happening) ______ in other places, too, are very difficult to solve.
6. The efforts (which are being made) ______ by various African governments aren't enough.
7. The wildlife conservation (= Erhaltung) (which is being carried out) ______ in Africa at the moment won't save many of the animals (that are threatened) ______ by man.
8. The rain forest (that is being burned) ______ in South America causes all sorts of problems for the animals there, too.
9. In 1989 in Kenya, 83-year-old George Adamson was killed by poachers – the man (who was murdered) ______ by the *shifta* (bandits) was the world's greatest lion expert. The lions (which had been protected) ______ by him so well for years are now in great danger.

5 **Setzen Sie jeweils eine passende Wendung mit Partizip ein.**

health permitting *provided that* *considering that* *judging by/from*

generally speaking *weather permitting* ~~*roughly speaking*~~ *talking of*

When Gareth Patterson arrived in Mashatu there were, *roughly speaking* [1] , 50–60 lions in the game reserve. Now there are 25 left and, ______ [2] the speed at which the others were killed, the last 25 will soon be gone as well. Life can be hard for a game warden in Mashatu but, ______ [3] (and most wardens in Mashatu are pretty healthy, of course), they do the job for many years. ______ [4], the average ranger is underpaid ______ [5] his work is difficult and often very dangerous. The climate can cause problems but, ______ [6], it's usually possible to drive around by jeep most of the year. And, ______ [7] the weather, it's often possible even in the rainy season – ______ [8] the roads haven't been completely washed away, that is!

9 RELATIVSÄTZE

Thema: Sherlock Holmes

9.1 Bestimmende Relativsätze

Read the examples

1. Crime is a theme **that/which** interests everybody.
2. The man **that/who** invented Holmes was Conan Doyle.
3. Holmes is a character **whose** name most people know.
4. A novel about him was the first book **(that/which)** Doyle wrote.
5. This is the poison **(that/which)** Moriarty killed her **with**.
6. This is the poison **with which** Moriarty killed her.

Remember

Ein bestimmender Relativsatz bezieht sich auf ein Wort und bestimmt dieses Wort genauer, indem er klarmacht, wer oder was gemeint ist.

Bei Personen steht that, who, whose (dessen, deren) ❷ ❸. Bei Dingen steht that, which, whose ❶ ❹. (That verwendet man außerdem nach all, anything, everything, nothing, something.)

Sind that, who, which **Objekt** im Relativsatz, kann man sie weglassen ❹ ❺.

Eine **Präposition** in einem bestimmenden Relativsatz steht vorzugsweise am **Ende des Relativsatzes** ❺ und weniger oft vor dem Relativpronomen ❻.

Beachten Sie: Bei einem bestimmenden Relativsatz werden keine Kommas gesetzt.

1 Eine der spannendsten Geschichten über Sherlock Holmes heißt *The Hound of the Baskervilles*.

Lesen Sie die Zusammenfassung der Handlung sorgfältig durch und verbinden Sie dann die darauffolgenden Satzteile miteinander.

One of Holmes' most famous cases is known as *The Hound of the Baskervilles*. It appeared as a novel in 15 chapters in *The Strand Magazine* from August 1901 to April 1902. Sir Charles Baskerville is discovered one night, dead from shock and terror, in the garden of his country house in Devon. Near the body are the footprints of a huge dog! The Baskervilles have lived under the curse (= Fluch) of a giant hound since 1648, when the wicked (= böse) Hugo Baskerville was killed by such an animal – his mysterious death was never fully explained. The nephew of Sir Charles, Henry Baskerville, is a rational man. He does not believe the legend and decides to go and live in his uncle's country house.

Holmes, busy with other cases, at first sends his friend Watson with Henry Baskerville to investigate. After many adventures Holmes and Watson solve the mystery, and Holmes is able to save the life of his client by shooting the hound when it attacks Henry Baskerville. (Most people, by the way, can't fall asleep if they read the book after going to bed!)

Welche Satzteile gehören zusammen?

1. *The Hound of the Baskervilles* is a case
2. It's actually a novel
3. It was *The Strand Magazine*
4. The footprints ... are clearly those of an enormous dog.
5. The shock ... is caused by a huge hound.
6. Sir Charles is one of the last of a family
7. Hugo was the wicked man
8. Hugo Baskerville's death was a mystery and remained something
9. Henry Baskerville is a rational man
10. The person ... is not Holmes but Watson.
11. Anybody ... will find it hard to sleep!

a discovered near the body of Sir Charles
b Sir Charles Baskerville dies from
c who originally brought the curse upon the Baskervilles in 1648.
d that could never be fully explained.
e who refuses to accept the legend of the hound.
f that investigates things at the start
g which is one of Holmes' most famous.
h in which the story first appeared from 1901–1902.
i whose members have lived under a terrible curse.
j published at the start of this century.
k who reads the book in bed at night

1. *g* 2. ___ 3. ___ 4. ___ 5. ___ 6. ___ 7. ___ 8. ___ 9. ___ 10. ___ 11. ___

2 Es gibt gewisse Figuren, die immer wieder in den Sherlock-Holmes-Geschichten vorkommen – einige davon sind fast so bekannt wie der große Detektiv selbst.

Setzen Sie that, which, who, whose nur da ein, wo es tatsächlich notwendig ist. Manchmal ist mehr als eine Lösung möglich.

1. The woman *that/who* is Holmes' housekeeper (= Haushälterin) at 221 B Baker Street is Mrs Hudson. She's a lady ___ natural kindness shows itself in the way ___ she looks after Holmes and Watson.
2. The friend ___ helps Holmes in the many adventures ___ occur (= passieren) is Dr John Watson.
3. Sherlock Holmes has a brother, Mycroft. It is Mycroft ___ mind is as brilliant as Sherlock's, but ___ ambitions as a detective are

limited: The job ______ he has as a special government adviser interests him more.

4. Holmes' greatest enemy is Professor Moriarty, a wicked genius ______ Holmes kills at the Reichenbach Falls near Meiringen in Switzerland. It's a fight ______ everybody at first believes Holmes to have died in as well.

9.2 Nicht bestimmende Relativsätze

Read the examples

❶ Dr Watson, **who** is Holmes' best friend, is based on Conan Doyle's private secretary.
❷ 221 B Baker Street, **which** is in central London, really exists.
❸ Conan Doyle – **whose** profession was that of a doctor – gave his hero many of his own characteristics.
❹ Every reader knows Professor Moriarty, **who** Holmes fights to the death **against**. (formell: **against whom** Holmes ... .)
❺ Conan Doyle managed to solve several real crimes, **which** helped to make him famous.

Remember

Ein nicht bestimmender Relativsatz enthält lediglich zusätzliche Informationen. Im Gegensatz zu einem bestimmenden Relativsatz braucht man einen nicht bestimmenden Relativsatz nicht, um zu verstehen, wer oder was gemeint ist. Lässt man ihn in den Sätzen oben weg, bleibt trotzdem eine sinnvolle Aussage übrig.

Bei Personen steht who, whose ❶ ❸; bei Dingen which, whose ❷ ❸. (That darf **nicht** in einem nicht bestimmenden Relativsatz stehen!)

Das Relativpronomen whom steht nur in formellem Englisch nach einer Präposition. In gesprochenem Englisch wird who verwendet und die Präposition ans Satzende gestellt ❹.

Das Relativpronomen kann sich auf einen ganzen vorausgehenden Satz beziehen und wird im Deutschen mit „was" übersetzt ❺.

Beachten Sie: Bei einem nicht bestimmenden Relativsatz werden immer Kommas (oder Gedankenstriche) gesetzt.

3 Sherlock Holmes ist unter anderem so beliebt, weil er viele interessante, exzentrische Angewohnheiten hat.

Setzen Sie jeweils das richtige Relativpronomen sowie alle Kommas ein.

1. Holmes keeps his pipe tobacco, *which* he seems to smoke the whole time, in a Persian (= persisch) slipper.
2. But his cigars ________ appear less often in the stories than his pipe are kept in a coal scuttle (= Kohlenschütte) ________ is certainly a very strange habit to have.
3. Holmes is, in fact, the author of a short book on tobacco in ________ he describes 140 different varieties.
4. He sometimes takes drugs like morphine (= Morphium) ________ is a sure sign that he's feeling bored.
5. Dr Watson ________ Holmes shares a large apartment with is a complete contrast to his friend: Watson to ________ Holmes seems like a genius is intelligent but in no way brilliant.
6. Watson is at times annoyed at his companion ________ habit of playing his violin at all hours keeps him awake at night.
7. When Holmes is working on a case ________ is most of the time he may spend days in bed thinking. And so his rooms ________ windows are rarely opened are usually full of tobacco smoke.

4 **Übersetzen Sie die Wörter in Klammern, indem Sie jeweils eine Lösung mit Präposition und Relativpronomen einsetzen. Verwenden Sie ein Relativpronomen nur da, wo es tatsächlich notwendig ist.**

1. (mit dem Holmes viele Abenteuer teilt)

   Dr Watson, *who Holmes shares many adventures with* , plays a role in all of the stories.
2. (in denen der große Detektiv erscheint)

   The first short stories, ________ , were published in 1891.

3. (mit dessen Namen Holmes immer verbunden (= connected) sein wird)

Conan Doyle, ______________________________ ,

was at first rather bored by his hero.

4. (gegen den Holmes kämpft)

Professor Moriarty, ______________________ , is his greatest enemy.

5 Bei welchem Satz kann man das Relativpronomen ganz weglassen?

______

10 ADVERBIEN

Thema: Movies

10.1 Adverbien mit zwei Formen

Read the examples

1. The film was **pretty** (= ziemlich) hopeless, but at least the star dressed **prettily** (= hübsch).
2. She works so **hard** (= schwer, hart) that she **hardly** (= kaum) has time to go to the cinema anymore.

Remember

Einige Adverbien haben zwei verschiedene Formen, wobei jede Form eine eigene Bedeutung hat. Die wichtigsten sind:

close	nahe (heran)	closely	genau (beobachten)
deep	tief	deeply	zutiefst
direct	direkt	directly	gleich, sofort
fair	fair	fairly	ziemlich
free	umsonst	freely	frei, freimütig
high	hoch (hinauf)	highly	höchst
just	nur gerade	justly	gerecht
late	spät	lately	in letzter Zeit
most	am meisten	mostly	meistens
near	nahe (heran)	nearly	beinahe, fast
(run) short	knapp (werden)	shortly	bald
wide	weit (auf)	widely (known)	allgemein (bekannt)

1 Unter Filmfans und -kritikern gelten eine Reihe von Filmen ganz einfach als „the world's worst movies". Hier sind einige Kommentare eines Kritikers über *Bedtime for Bonzo* (1951) und dessen Star, Ronald Reagan, den ehemaligen US-Präsidenten, der 2004 verstarb.

Vervollständigen Sie die Sätze durch ein Adverb mit oder ohne -ly.

You'll have a chance to see *Bedtime for Bonzo* *shortly* [1] (short) – it's on TV next week. It's usually shown ________ [2] (late) at night, but any film with the ex-president in it is ________ [3] (high) interesting to lots of people. In fact, ________ [4] (late) Mr Reagan's movies – ________ [5] (most) the bad ones! – have been attracting even more viewers than when he was president. It's ________ [6] (wide) known that your environment can influence your intelligence. In the film, a professor (Ronald Reagan) and his wife raise (= erziehen) a chimpanzee in their home to test this. Reagan acts the part ________ [7] (fair) well, but critics haven't treated him quite ________ [8] (just) by saying that the real star is Bonzo! Reagan speaks to Bonzo like an old friend, giving him food every time he goes ________ [9] (near) him. And Bonzo opens his mouth ________ [10] (wide) when Ronnie comes ________ [11] (close). He's a ________ [12] (pretty) clever chimp (Bonzo, that is). But we must play ________ [13] (fair) with the ex-president and admit that the script (= Drehbuch) isn't too good. But this isn't ________ [14] (just) another silly film – it's one of the silliest ever and, of its type, ________ [15] (near) perfect. So don't miss it!

10.2 Verb anstatt Adverb

Read the examples

1. Film stars **are known to** earn huge amounts. (... verdienen bekanntlich ...)
2. **I'm afraid I used to** drink far too much. (Leider trank ich früher ...)

Remember

Eine Reihe von gängigen Adverbien im Deutschen haben als Entsprechung im Englischen recht häufig ein Verb ❶ ❷. Die bekanntesten sind:

allmählich	get, grow
anscheinend	appear, seem
dauernd	keep on
gern	like
hoffentlich	hope, it's hoped/let's hope
lieber	prefer
nämlich	you know, you see
offenbar	appear, seem
sicher	be certain/sure
vermutlich	presume, suppose
vielleicht	may, might
wahrscheinlich	be likely to
weiter(hin)	go/keep on
zufällig	happen to

2 Im Jahre 1933 erschien in den USA der erste Film über einen Riesengorilla namens King Kong. Der Gorilla selbst wurde schnell zu einer Art Volksheld. Es gab unzählige Neuverfilmungen, darunter ein totaler, sehr teurer Flop aus dem Jahr 1976 sowie ein großer Erfolg aus dem Jahr 2005.

Übersetzen Sie jeweils die Wörter in Klammern durch ein passendes englisches Verb anstelle des deutschen Adverbs. Manchmal ist mehr als eine Lösung möglich.

1. A group of American scientists *happen to discover* (zufällig entdecken) an enormous gorilla on a Pacific island.
2. The gorilla ______ (wohnt anscheinend) somewhere among the mountains on the island.

3. King Kong is captured, but the audience soon realizes that he ________ (wahrscheinlich nicht ... bleibt) in his cage.
4. The giant ape is transported to the USA on a ship, where he ________ (dauernd versucht, ... zu brechen) his chains.
5. On the way to the USA Kong ________ (verliebt sich offenbar = fall in love with) a young woman on the ship – she, ________ (nämlich), is the only person on board that feels sorry for him.
6. Gorillas ________ (sind bekanntlich) very gentle (= sanftmütig) animals, but Kong is the cinema's first gorilla lover!
7. The affair between the beautiful woman and the hairy ape is so silly that some people ________ (vielleicht anfangen werden zu lachen).
8. Anyway, you ________ (werden ... sicher genießen) the 1976 version ... if you like comedies!

10.3 Inversion

Read the examples

❶ Only once **did a King Kong film earn** a lot of money.
❷ Never **have they made** a worse horror movie.
❸ **Out went** the lights, and **in came** Dracula.
(Aber: **Out they** went, and **in he** came.)

Remember

Bestimmte Adverbien und Adverbialbestimmungen mit einschränkender oder negativer Bedeutung können am Satzanfang stehen, wenn sie besonders betont werden sollen. Eine Inversion gilt heutzutage im Englischen als formell und wird in Zeitungsberichten, Rundfunknachrichten usw. verwendet. Die Wortstellung in solchen Sätzen entspricht der eines Fragesatzes ❶ ❷. Zu diesen Adverbien und Adverbialbestimmungen gehören: hardly, in no way, never, no sooner ... than, not only, not until (tomorrow, ...), nowhere, only (once ...), rarely, scarcely (kaum), seldom (selten), under no circumstances.

Adverbien wie back, down, here, in, out, over, round, there, up erscheinen im Alltagsgebrauch häufig am Satzanfang ❸. Aber dies ist nur beim *simple present* und *simple past* möglich. Ist das Subjekt ein Substantiv, so steht es hinter dem Verb.

3 Schreiben Sie diese Sätze neu. Bilden Sie jeweils eine Inversion, indem Sie den Satz mit dem Adverb oder der Adverbialbestimmung im unterstrichenen Teil beginnen.

1. The fifties (= die fünfziger Jahre) had no sooner arrived than Hollywood began making science-fiction films.

   No sooner had the fifties arrived than Hollywood began making science-fiction films.
2. Hollywood rarely made good horror movies in the fifties.

   ______ good horror movies in the fifties.
3. There has seldom been a movie as funny as *Teenagers from Outer Space* (1959).

   ______

   as funny as *Teenagers from Outer Space* (1959).
4. It didn't become a cult film until recently.

   ______ a cult film.
5. A spaceship comes down to Earth and, as a hatch (= Luke) goes up, some teenagers from another galaxy get out.

   ______ to Earth and, as a hatch goes up

   ______ from another galaxy.

10.4 Adjektive anstatt Adverbien

Read the examples

❶ The results of the survey look **surprising**.
❷ It's becoming **difficult** for him to find good roles to play.
❸ The plot (= Handlung) was **bad** and the actors were **dreadful**.

Remember

Mit den Verben appear, be, feel, look, seem, smell, sound, taste und mit allen Verben, die dem deutschen „werden“ entsprechen (become, get, go, grow), verwendet man im Englischen ein Adjektiv anstatt eines Adverbs ❶–❸.

4 Vervollständigen Sie diese Publicitysprüche und Rezensionen dreier Hollywoodfilme mit einem Adjektiv oder Adverb.

1. In Elvis Presley's latest movie, *Paradise Hawaiian Style*, 'The King' looks *irresistible* (irresistible = unwiderstehlich) as usual! The songs sound ________ (great) and Elvis acts his role ________ (fantastic) from start to finish!
2. *Attack of the Fifty-Foot Woman* isn't a film you can take ________ (serious). ________ (simple) anything can happen in it! You might think you're going ________ (crazy) when you see a fifty-foot woman destroying a town! And if that sounds ________ (unbelievable) or seems ________ (impossible), then go and see it ________ (fast) – the whole thing is so ________ (awful) that it won't be showing much longer.
3. Watching *Robot Monster* is like eating in a cheap restaurant where the food tastes ________ (horrible) and smells ________ (terrible). Ugh! It grows so ________ (dull = eintönig) at times that I saw one person fall asleep watching it. The hero, a gorilla monster from another planet, seems to feel ________ (tired) of it all from the start. The plot is ________ (unrealistic); the characters never behave ________ (sensible). It shouldn't be shown ________ (public); they ought to throw it into the ocean!

11 PHRASAL VERBS

Thema: Development aid

11.1 Verwendung

Read the example

Why have they **turned down** the offer of US aid? Can they still **carry out** all their development projects?

Remember

Phrasal verbs werden häufig in der Umgangssprache bevorzugt. Sie bestehen aus einem **Verb** in Kombination mit einem **Adverb** wie ahead, away, back, down, off, out, over, round, through, up.

Manchmal setzt sich ein *phrasal verb* auch aus **Verb + Adverb + Präposition** zusammen, z. B.: do away with (loswerden), keep up with (Schritt halten mit), get along with (mit jdm. auskommen) - siehe die Liste der *phrasal verbs* auf S. 96–97.

Manche Verben können mit verschiedenen Adverbien kombiniert werden, z. B.: turn on (einschalten), turn over (umblättern, -drehen), turn up (auftauchen, lauter stellen).

Oft ergibt sich die Bedeutung eines *phrasal verb* automatisch aus den einzelnen Bestandteilen, aber in vielen Fällen lässt sich eine Bedeutung nur schwer erschließen, z. B. give in (nachgeben).

1 Hier sind Informationen über Entwicklungshilfeprojekte und -probleme des fiktiven Staates Vanaratu.

Setzen Sie jeweils das passende *phrasal verb* in die Sätze ein. Manchmal müssen Sie dabei auch auf die richtige Verbform achten. (Die Liste auf S. 96–97 hilft Ihnen dabei.)

queue up | *point out* | *tear down* | ~~*build up*~~ | *do away with* | *break off* | *set up* | *wake up* | *carry out* | *dry up* | *keep up with*

1. So far, Vanaratu has not been able to *build up* its only resource: its still small oil industry.
2. It will take about five years to ______ a modern school system in every part of Vanaratu.

3. One important fact must be ______ : the country has very few trained teachers.
4. The Vanaratu Government intends to ______ its ambitious plan to ______ all the slums in the capital.
5. The attempts (= Versuch) to ______ corruption and destroy it forever have been a fiasco.
6. Vanaratu cannot hope to ______ the speed of development in other parts of the world. But the country is beautiful, and tourists will soon ______ in their thousands to buy tickets for a holiday here.
7. One problem is that there has been little rain for three years, and some of the big rivers may soon ______.
8. But the nation's biggest problem is that last year it decided to ______ relations with the USA. That ended USA aid. Vanaratu must ______ from its sleep and face the realities of the modern world.

11.2 Wortstellung

Read the examples

❶ Our task is to **build up** our oil industry.
❷ Our task is to **build** our oil industry **up**.
❸ Our task is to **build** it **up**.
❹ Our task is to **build up** the oil industry and tourism.

Remember

Ist das Objekt eines *phrasal verb* ein **Substantiv**, so steht das *phrasal verb* entweder vor diesem Substantiv ❶ oder es teilt sich und steht davor und dahinter ❷.
Wenn das Objekt aber ein **Pronomen** ist, teilt sich das *phrasal verb* immer und steht vor und hinter dem Pronomen ❸.
Wenn das Objekt **lang** ist, wird das *phrasal verb* nicht getrennt und steht vor dem Objekt ❹.

2 Entwicklungshilfe für die Dritte Welt ist oft ein umstrittenes Thema. Die britische Zeitschrift *Independent Times* hat dazu einige Leute auf der Straße interviewt.

Vervollständigen Sie die Sätze mit den Wörtern in Klammern. Das Verb müssen Sie jeweils ergänzen, um ein passendes *phrasal verb* einsetzen zu können. Achten Sie besonders auf die Wortstellung. Es sind manchmal zwei Lösungen möglich, aber es genügt, wenn Sie eine angeben.

1. Development aid is a lot of nonsense – why should we *give away millions/give millions away* (millions/give) every year for nothing?
2. I'm sick of those countries taking our money and I won't ______ (the situation/put) much longer!
3. We in Britain have an obligation to help now – we mustn't ______ (it/put) a moment longer.
4. When those nations were colonies we were happy to ______ (their natural resources = Bodenschätze; take) and use them for ourselves. But now we must ______ (them/give) again as development aid.
5. The industrial nations should learn to ______ (the poor nations/get) – just the way good friends should.
6. Even if aid costs us a lot, I think we ought to ______ (it/keep) and not reduce it.
7. Nobody can ______ (the mess/clear) in the Third World!
8. I don't care about the poor countries – and if we've got treaties (= Verträge) with them, we should ______ (them all/tear)!
9. We must never refuse to help; we must never ______ (requests for aid/turn).

Liste der *phrasal verbs*

beat up	zusammenschlagen
break off	abbrechen
breathe in	einatmen
breathe out	ausatmen
bring up	erziehen
build up	aufbauen
call in	vorbeikommen
call out	ausrufen
calm down	(sich) beruhigen
carry out	durchführen
check in	sich anmelden, abfertigen lassen
cheer up	aufheitern
clean up	aufräumen
clear up	aufräumen, sich aufklären
close down	schließen
come back	zurückkommen
come in	hereinkommen
come up	herankommen
do away with	loswerden
dry up	ab-, austrocknen
fall over	hinfallen
fill in/out	ausfüllen
fill up	(auf)füllen
find out	herausfinden
get ahead	vorankommen
get along with	(miteinander) auskommen
get away	entkommen
get in/on	einsteigen (in)
get off/out	aussteigen (aus)
get on with	(mit etwas) weitermachen
get up	aufstehen
give away	weggeben
give in	nachgeben
go back	zurückgehen
go off	fortgehen
go on	weitergehen, fortfahren
go out	ausgehen
go up	steigen
grow up	auf-, heranwachsen
keep up	beibehalten
keep up with	Schritt halten mit
knock down	abreißen
knock out	k. o. schlagen
leave out	aus-, weglassen
look up	nachschlagen
make up	sich ausdenken
mess up	vermasseln
pick up	aufheben, mitbekommen

point out	hinweisen auf
put away	wegräumen
put off	aufschieben
put on	anziehen
put through	durchstellen
put up	aufstellen, erhöhen
put up with sth.	sich mit etw. abfinden
queue up	sich anstellen
ring up	anrufen
run out (of)	zu Ende gehen, ausgehen
set off	aufbrechen
set up	errichten, etablieren
settle down	sich niederlassen
settle in	sich einleben
show off	angeben
sit down	sich setzen
speak up	lauter sprechen
stand up	aufstehen
start off	beginnen
stay up	aufbleiben
switch off	ab-, ausschalten
switch on	einschalten
take away	wegnehmen
take back	zurücknehmen

take down	abnehmen
take in	aufnehmen, betrügen
take off	ausziehen, starten
take out	herausnehmen
take over	übernehmen
tear down	abreißen
tear up	zerreißen
turn down	leiser stellen, ablehnen
turn off	ab-, ausschalten
turn on	einschalten
turn over	umblättern, -drehen
turn up	lauter stellen
wake up	aufwachen, -wecken
wash up	abwaschen
work out	ausrechnen, -arbeiten
write down	auf-, niederschreiben

12 DER BESTIMMTE ARTIKEL

Thema: How a politician uses facts

Read the examples

1. **Lunch** is my favourite meal.
2. **The lunch** she made was awful.
3. Hans will climb **Mount Ararat** in **Turkey** in **September**.
4. Cathy will move to **Steinsdorf Street** on **the Isar River** in **summer**.
5. She's from **the United States** and loves hiking in **the Himalayas**.

Remember

Meistens werden Substantive, die in einem allgemeinen Sinn verwendet werden, nicht mit dem bestimmten Artikel verwendet ①.

Wenn das Substantiv nicht allgemein verwendet wird, sondern etwas ganz Bestimmtes bezeichnet, verwendet man den bestimmten Artikel ②.

Leider hat diese allgemeine Regel für die Verwendung des bestimmten Artikels viele Ausnahmen. Meistens stehen Eigennamen ohne Artikel, z. B. Personen, Berge, Länder und Monate ③, Straßen und Jahreszeiten ④. Flüsse dagegen stehen mit Artikel ④ und auch geografische Bezeichnungen in der Mehrzahl ⑤.

Einige wichtige Ausnahmen sind: all the clothes, on the phone, most people, in case, play the piano/guitar etc., on TV, on the radio.

1 Politiker müssen in der Lage sein, über die unterschiedlichsten Fakten und über bestimmte Tatsachen reden zu können. Senatorin Everywoman hat Glück, dass ihre ausgezeichneten Mitarbeiter allgemeine Daten und Tatsachen für sie zusammentragen.

Lesen Sie diese Aussagen durch und entscheiden Sie, welche Substantive in einem allgemeinen und welche in einem bestimmten Sinn verwendet werden. Setzen Sie dann entsprechend den bestimmten Artikel ein.

1. I'll speak to *the* [1] steelworker's union on ________ [2] last Wednesday in June.
2. Usually, ________ [3] Wednesday evening is a good time to speak at ________ [4] union (= Gewerkschaft) meetings.
3. An important issue for this city is ________ [5] pollution.
4. Ladies and gentlemen, ________ [6] pollution of the Susko River is of great concern to us all.

5. Look at ______ [7] flowers on that table over there, Mr Botan. Aren't they a rare type of orchid?
6. Mr Botan's favourite topic of conversation is ______ [8] flowers.
7. Of course ______ [9] aftershave I gave to you was my idea, darling!
8. Why do you ask? ______ [10] A/aftershave is usually a good present for your husband's birthday.
9. It's important for a person in your position to go to ______ [11] church.
10. My family and I are so happy to be here at ______ [12] First Presbyterian Church of Wauseon this morning.
11. By the way, Mrs Jackson, I thought that ______ [13] violence in ______ [14] *Indiana Jones*' films was terrible.
12. Mrs Jackson is opposed to ______ [15] violence in ______ [16] films for ______ [17] young people.
13. Mr Fisk hates ______ [18] spaghetti but he loves ______ [19] salad.
14. ______ [20] S/spaghetti in this bistro isn't very good, Mr Fisk, but I can recommend ______ [21] salad.

2 Senatorin Everywoman muss natürlich auch Briefe an ihre Wähler schreiben können, oft auf die seltsamsten Anfragen hin. In diesem Antwortbrief an die Vereinigung der Artischockenzüchter im Landkreis Pocohontas nimmt sie die Einladung an, eine Rede auf deren Jahresversammlung zu halten.

Setzen Sie den bestimmten Artikel in den Brief ein, aber nur, wo er unverzichtbar ist.

Dear Friends,

It is with ______ [1] great pleasure that I accept your kind invitation to speak at *the* [2] 22nd Annual Convention (= Fachkonferenz) of ______ [3] Artichoke Growers of ______ [4] Pocohontas County. ______ [5] C/conventions of this sort are so essential to ______ [6] growth of ______ [7] information and _____ [8] understanding among all of _____ [9] agricultural experts in this area. _____ [10] A/artichoke growers of _____ [11] Pocohontas County have always been one of _____ [12] most vital forces in _____ [13] county's economy, and in _____ [14] economy of _____ [15] whole state. I am especially pleased that you have chosen for _____ [16] theme this year ' _____ [17] *C/crime in* _____ [18] *Artichoke Fields*'. _____ [19] E/environmental protection is a special interest of mine, and I will include in my speech a list of _____ [20] shocking environmental crimes committed in _____ [21] county this past year. We all need to get to _____ [22] work fighting these crimes, even though _____ [23] work is frustrating.

In addition let me say, _____ [24] farmers have always been _____ [25] backbone of _____ [26] nation's strength. And _____ [27] farmers of _____ [28] Pocohontas County are no exception to _____ [29] rule. _____ [30] V/vegetables are as important a natural resource as _____ [31] oil or _____ [32] coal. And _____ [33] vegetables grown in Pocohontas County are among _____ [34] best.

By _____ [35] way, your exhibition (= Ausstellung) of vegetables grown near _____ [36] Susko River and around _____ [37] Mt Tanaho was very interesting, probably one of _____ [38] most interesting of its kind in _____ [39] United States. I am looking forward to _____ [40] lunch scheduled after _____ [41] programme.

I assume (= annehmen) that _____ [42] artichokes being served are from _____ [43] Pocohontas County, as _____ [44] artichokes are my favourite food!

All the best to you!

Ellen Everywoman

13 MENGENANGABEN

Thema: Student life

13.1 *A/an, some, any, every, each*

Read the examples

1. Here's **an** article about **a** student in the UK with **some** interesting information about student life there.
2. This student had to pay 30 Euros **an** hour for private tutoring.
3. There are **some** interesting facts here about student aid. Shall I read you **some**?
4. There isn't **anything** here about university entrance requirements.
5. Have you got **any** brochures about the requirements in the UK?
6. Can **anybody** go to university in the UK?
7. **Every** university student there has to have A-levels or **any** other equivalent higher education entrance qualification.
8. **Each** student should decide for him or herself which is the best subject to study.
9. But not **every** student **is** able to find an immediate opening to study **their** chosen major subject at the university **they** choose.
10. **Nobody** in our family has ever studied abroad, but there's **nothing** to stop you from doing it.

Remember

Den unbestimmten Artikel a benutzt man mit Wörtern, die mit Konsonantlauten anfangen, an mit Wörtern, die mit Vokallauten anfangen ❶.

A oder an wird auch zusammen mit Angaben über Maß und Zeit verwendet und entspricht dann dem deutschen „in der/dem“: 20 km **an** hour = 20 km in der Stunde ❷.

Some und die Ableitungen von some (somebody, something usw.) verwendet man vorwiegend in bejahten Aussagesätzen, entweder allein oder vor Substantiven, die Unzählbares ausdrücken ❶, und vor Substantiven in der Mehrzahl ❸, außerdem, wenn man etwas anbietet ❸.

Beachten Sie: Es gibt einige gängige Begriffe, die im Deutschen die Mehrzahl bilden, im Englischen jedoch nicht. Beispiele dafür sind information, knowledge, experience (= Erfahrung(en)), data. Diese werden als unzählbare Substantive mit some/any and dem Verb in der 3. Person Singular benutzt ❶.

Any und die Ableitungen von any (anyone, anything usw.) werden hauptsächlich in verneinten Aussagesätzen verwendet ❹ und in Fragen, wenn die Existenz von etwas erfragt wird ❺. Seltener wird es verwendet, um „jede, egal welche“ auszudrücken ❻.

Man verwendet every und die Ableitungen davon, wenn jeder (Person oder Sache) in einer Gruppe gemeint ist. Es wird immer mit einem Verb in der 3. Person Singular verwendet ❾.
Each betont jede einzelne Person oder Sache in einer bestimmten Gruppe ❽.

No one und nobody bedeuten „niemand“ und werden als Singularpronomen verwendet. Nothing bedeutet „nichts“ und bezeichnet eine unzählbare Menge ❿.

1 Wählen Sie die beste Satzergänzung und streichen Sie die unpassenden Wörter durch.

1. I need an/every/some information about universities in the UK.
2. There isn't anything/everything/something in our school about it.
3. Each thing/Something/Everything you need to know about the subject was/were in a/an article I found on the Internet.
4. You don't need to look up anything/everything/nothing else.
5. Our school paper interviewed any/each/every student in the 12th grade about his or her individual plans for the coming year.
6. Have you had an/any/some experience/experiences with a/an university abroad?
7. Some/Any/Every students in our class told us about doing the 11th grade in a secondary school in another country.
8. But of course nobody/everybody/anybody has no/any/some direct knowledge/knowledges about higher education.
9. I'd love to spend a/an year abroad. It doesn't really matter where – everywhere/somewhere/anywhere will do.
10. I've got every/any/some great books on study abroad at home. Would you like every/any/some?

13.2 *Many, a lot of, much, more, most, few, fewer, fewest, little, less, least*

Read the examples

❶ There are **a lot of** good books in this library, but **not many** students here use them for research.
❷ Libraries are great places for people with **a lot of** time, but not **much** money.
❸ In the town where I used to live they had **many more** people using the libraries, and also **much more** trouble with lost books.
❹ There are **a few** computers in our library, but **very few** that are fast enough, and even **fewer** with enough capacity.
❺ There is very **little** interest here in good reading materials, and even **less** interest in encyclopedias.
❻ There**'s quite a lot of** space here in John's flat, but there **are also quite a few** people at this party. It's really crowded!
❼ **The most** time I've ever spent in a library was six hours.
❽ **Most** libraries are not open on Sundays.
❾ **Most of the** time I spent in libraries was very interesting.

Remember

Bei zählbaren Mengen (d. h., wenn man eine Zahl sinnvoll vor das Substantiv setzen kann), verwendet man sowohl a lot of/lots of als auch (a) few in bejahten Sätzen ❶. Das Gleiche gilt für die Steigerungsformen dieser Pronomen (more, most, fewer, fewest) ❸ ❹. In verneinten Sätzen und Fragen steht many ❶.
Beachten Sie: Few kann mehrere Bedeutungen haben: a few = einige, few/very few = wenige/sehr wenige ❹. Dagegen heißt „ziemlich viel" bei zählbaren Mengen quite a few ❻.

Bei nicht zählbaren Mengen verwendet man a lot of/lots of und (a) little in bejahten Sätzen ❷ ❺. Das Gleiche gilt für die Steigerungsformen dieser Pronomen (more, most, less, least) ❸ ❺. In verneinten Sätzen und Fragen steht much ❷.

Most als Mengenbezeichnung steht mit dem bestimmten Artikel, wenn es superlativische Bedeutung hat ❼. Ohne Artikel steht es aber, wenn es „fast alle/der größere Teil" in einem allgemeinen Sinn bedeutet ❽.
Most of the ..., wie all of the ..., some of the ..., none of the ... usw., wird verwendet, wenn das folgende Substantiv sich auf etwas Bestimmtes bezieht. Vor most of ... steht **kein** Artikel ❾.

2 Setzen Sie die passende Mengenangabe ein.

1. (Viele) *A lot of* students in our town decide to share a flat because it costs (sehr wenig) ______.
2. (Die meisten) ______ students are happy to share a flat because they haven't got (viel) ______ money and it's often (viel) ______ fun.
3. (Die meisten) ______ landlords (= Vermieter) in our area don't mind renting a flat to (einige) ______ students together.
4. There were (ziemlich viel) ______ flats available in the paper last week, but there weren't (viele) ______ inexpensive ones.
5. (Alle) ______ flats we could afford just had (zu wenig) ______ space for five people to share.
6. (Das meiste) ______ money I ever spent on a flat as a student was € 300 a month.
7. There are always (einige) ______ problems with a shared flat, but (die meiste) ______ time there are (ziemlich viele) ______ advantages.
8. Like in any home, there's always (zu viel) ______ housework and (zu wenig) ______ time to do it, or perhaps just (zu wenige) ______ people willing to take on (viel) ______ responsibility for it.

3 Bill ist ein amerikanischer Student, der dieses Jahr in einer europäischen Stadt studiert.

Schauen Sie sich seine Ausgaben für September und Oktober an und ergänzen Sie die Sätze.

	September	**October**
Tuition (= Studiengebühren)	€ 750	
Books, photocopies, etc.	€ 150	€ 30
Rent (share of flat)	€ 330	€ 330
Food	€ 340	€ 280
Transport	€ 75	€ 30
Telephone, post	€ 30	€ 65
University events	€ 15	
Leisure activities	€ 20	€ 15
Clothing, hygiene	€ 220	€ 20

1. Bill spent *(a lot/much) more* in September than in October.
2. He bought ______ books in October.
3. Both months he spent very ______ on leisure activities.
4. In September he spent just as ______ on rent as in October.
5. In September he needed the ______ money for tuition.
6. He needed the ______ money for university events.
7. He spent ______ money on transport in October than in September.
8. Probably because it was the beginning of the school year, he bought ______ clothes in September, and ______ in October.
9. He must have made quite ______ phone calls in October.

TEST

Mixed exercises 1

1 Setzen Sie die richtigen Verbformen ein.

1. For thousands of years man ______ (ask) the question 'What is time?'.
2. Babylonian astronomers ______ (know) the number of days in a year, but their priests ______ (insist) on 360 days – a 'magic' number.
3. The moon's cycle (= Zyklus) ______ (last) approximately 29 1/2 days, and the earth's 365 1/4 days.
4. In 200 million years a day ______ (last) 25 hours.
5. In the eleventh century a Chinese, Su Song, ______ (make) one of the first mechanical clocks – a water clock.
6. In the sixteenth century Galileo ______ (sit) in a church when he ______ (notice) a lantern swinging and ______ (discover) the pendulum (= Pendel).
7. Since the 1940s, scientists ______ (know) that the electrons of atoms oscillate (= pendeln) as regularly as a pendulum.
8. For some years scientists ______ (measure) time most accurately with atomic clocks.
9. – Hello! BTL Radio Station calling. Can you give me the time, please? – Just a moment. I ______ (check) the atomic clock.
10. Because of Einstein's theory of relativity we can predict that a rapidly moving clock ______ (tick) more slowly.
11. Three scientists in California ______ (start) a project to research time travel early next year.
12. Many science fiction fans believe that in a hundred years' time, people ______ ______ (use) time machines to travel back and forth in time.

13. However, most scientists agree that this probably ______ (not be) possible.

14. It is likely that most of the people you know ______ (wear) watches at this moment.

15. Men ______ (not start) to wear wrist watches until World War I.

16. The soldiers ______ (find) it difficult then to reach inside their uniform coats to check the time on a pocket watch.

17. Last Thursday I ______ (want) to give my mother a watch for her birthday, but I ______ (forget) to take my credit card with me when I was shopping on Wednesday.

18. Tomorrow, at 10 a.m., our tour bus ______ (leave) for a guided tour of the biggest Seiko watch factory in Japan.

19. Even as you read this, 1,150 robots ______ (assemble = zusammensetzen) watches there.

20. Every two seconds a new watch ______ (come) off the assembly line (= Fließband).

▶ 1 Die Zeiten

Your points: ______ /24

2 Setzen Sie die richtigen Verbformen im Passiv ein.

1. In 1884 Greenwich, England, ______ (choose) as the site (= Platz) of zero-degree longitude (= Längengrad).
2. Before this, Jerusalem, the Great Pyramid and Paris ______ ______ (consider) as possible sites.
3. The Greenwich site ______ (not/acknowledge) on French maps until 1914.
4. Today, time ______ (measure) in twenty-four global time zones.
5. Daylight saving time (= Sommerzeit) ______ (use) since 1915.

6. Just now, the problem of a unified daylight saving time in all European countries ______ ______ (discuss) in the European Parliament.
7. More than half a billion watches ______ (produce) every year all over the world.
8. Studies ______ (make) currently (= augenblicklich) on time travel.
9. The results of these studies ______ (not/know) for the next ten years at least.
10. The possibilities of time travel ______ (discuss) when I arrived at the dinner table yesterday evening.

▶ 2 Das Passiv **Your points:** ______ /10

3 Setzen Sie die richtigen Verbformen, auch im Passiv, ein.

Jaipur, India, 10 February

Dear Susan,

Harry and I ______ 1 (be) in India since 1 February, but I ______ ______ 2 (feel) as if we ______ 3 (be) here ten weeks. Since we ______ 4 (arrive), each day ______ 5 (fill) with so many new and interesting things!

We ______ 6 (start) our tour in Delhi on the 1st. There ______ ______ 7 (be) fascinating sights there, as Delhi ______ 8 (rule) (= beherrschen) by so many different cultures before Indian independence in 1947. I especially ______ 9 (like) the Red Fort, which ______ ______ 10 (built) by the Moghuls in the seventeenth century. Our next stop ______ ______ 11 (be) Agra on the 3rd. The train connection between Delhi and Agra is very good. The express train always ______ 12 (leave) at 7 a.m. and only ______ 13 (take) three hours. Agra was amazing! Harry ______ ______ 14 (be) there before in 1976 and 1985, but he ______ 15 (say) he ______ [16] (not see) it like that. When we ______ [17] (arrive) they ______ [18] (have) a festival called Holi, and people ______ [19] (run) through the streets and ______ [20] (throw) coloured water and powder at each other all day long. I ______ [21] (hit) twice by purple and turquoise water. I ______ [22] (look) like a peacock (= Pfau) at the end of the day. Our tour guide ______ [23] (have) my dress cleaned for me the next day, but I ______ [24] (not want) to make our group wait. The Taj Mahal ______ [25] (describe) and ______ [26] (photograph) so often over the years, but it ______ [27] (be) still an incredible experience to see it first-hand last week! On the way from Agra to Jaipur on the 5th, we ______ [28] (stop) in a deserted Moghul city called Fatephur Sikri. Marvellous – even though parts of it ______ [29] (renovate) at the moment, and can't ______ [30] (see) very well. Now we ______ [31] (be) in Jaipur, the 'pink city' since yesterday. Today I ______ [32] (not do) any sightseeing yet. Too exhausted! I ______ [33] (sit) in the hotel room, ______ [34] (write) letters, ______ [35] (draw), and ______ [36] (enjoy) the air conditioning since this morning! It ______ [37] (be) hot here! Tomorrow we ______ [38] (visit) a fort and palace near Jaipur called Amber, and the tour guide promises that we ______ [39] (take) there by elephant! Don't worry! I ______ [40] (not forget) to take a picture! ______ [41] (you/ever ride) an elephant, Susan? Actually, by the time this tour is finished, we ______

______ 42 (travel) by plane, train, bus, bicycle rickshaw, elephant and camel! It's hard to believe that just two weeks from now I ______ 43 (sit) opposite you again in the office in cold Manchester!

All the best to you, and love from

Alice

▶ 1 Die Zeiten, 2 Das Passiv

Your points: ______ /43

Mixed exercises 2

1 Lesen Sie diese berühmten Zitate und setzen Sie dann die unterstrichenen Wörter in die indirekte Rede ein.

1. Francis Bacon (1561–1626): "Hope is a good breakfast, but it is a bad supper."
   Francis Bacon said that hope ______ a good breakfast, but it ______ a bad supper.
2. Napoleon Bonaparte (1769–1821): "The bullet that is to kill me has not yet been moulded (= gegossen)."
   Napoleon claimed that the bullet that ______ to kill ______ ______ not yet been moulded.
3. Alexander (356–323 BC): "I am dying with the help of too many physicians."
   Alexander insisted that ______ ______ with the help of too many physicians.
4. Lord Nelson (1758–1805): "England expects every man will do his duty."
   Lord Nelson stated that England ______ every man ______ his duty.
5. Lord Nelson (his dying words): "I have done my duty."
   As Lord Nelson lay dying, he said that ______ ______ ______ duty.

6. Socrates (469–399 BC): "Bad men live to eat and drink, whereas good men eat and drink in order to live."

Socrates stated that bad men ______ to eat and drink, whereas good men ______ and ______ in order to live.

7. Mark Twain (1835–1910) (in a telegram to the Associated Press): "Reports of my death were greatly exaggerated (= übertrieben)."

Mark Twain cabled to the AP that reports of ______ death ______ ______ greatly exaggerated.

8. Ralph Waldo Emerson (1803–1882) (to Thoreau, in prison for not paying his taxes): "Why are you here?" Henry David Thoreau (1817–1862) (in answer to Emerson): "Why are you not here?"

When Thoreau was in prison for not paying his taxes, Emerson asked him why ______ ______ ______. In return, Thoreau questioned Emerson why ______ ______ ______.

9. Marcus Aurelius (121–180): "Everything that happens happens as it should, and if you observe carefully, you will find this to be so."

Marcus Aurelius insisted that everything that ______ ______ ______ as it should, and if you ______ carefully, you ______ this to be so.

10. Christopher North (1785–1854): "Laws were made to be broken."

Christopher North stated that laws ______ to be broken.

11. Abraham Lincoln (1809–1865): "You can fool all of the people some of the time, and you can fool some of the people all of the time. But you can't fool all of the people all the time."

Abraham Lincoln remarked that you ______ all of the people some of the time, and you ______ some of the people all of the time. But you ______ all of the people all of the time.

12. Archimedes (287–212 BC): “Eureka: I have found it!”

Archimedes exclaimed that ______ ______ it.

13. Mark Twain: “Training is everything. The peach was once a bitter almond (= Mandel), and a cauliflower (= Blumenkohl) is nothing but a cabbage with a college education.”

Mark Twain stated that training ______ everything. The peach ______ once a bitter almond and a cauliflower ______ ______ nothing but a cabbage with a college education.

14. George Bernard Shaw (1856–1950): “He who can, does. He who can’t, teaches.”

Shaw said that he who ______, ______, and he who ______, ______.

▶ **3 Die indirekte Rede** — Your points: ______ /40

2 **Diese Sätze über Katastrophen und Katastrophenmaßnahmen sind jeweils *if*-Sätze des Typs 1, 2 und 3. Vervollständigen Sie die Sätze.**

1. If people ______ (not panic) during a catastrophe, many problems could be avoided.
2. What ______ (you do) if your plane were hijacked (= entführt)?
3. If the planes in an international air show in 1988 ______ (follow) the rules, and ______ (not fly) so close to the spectators, a terrible accident could have been avoided.
4. Many trees were damaged in the hurricane (= Orkan) last weekend. ______ (be) careful if you ______ (walk) in the forest!
5. If your roof blew off in a hurricane, I’m not sure the insurance ______ ______ (pay) for it.
6. They ______ (lose) many valuable antiques if the flood waves ______ (reach) their shop last week!

7. If there ______ (be) storm warnings and I ______ (be) out on a lake in a sailing boat, I would bring in the boat immediately.
8. If the Titanic hadn't been travelling so fast, it probably ______ ______ (not hit) the iceberg.
9. Never ______ (use) the lift if fire ______ ______ (break) out in a high building.
10. If you ______ (live) in California, Japan or Mexico, you would think about earthquakes (= Erdbeben) more often.
11. If people in these countries ______ (not build) their houses correctly, they might break down during an earthquake.
12. Tall buildings ______ (survive) an average earthquake if they are built on the right kind of foundation.
13. If buildings had been constructed better in Mexico City, nine thousand people ______ ______ (not kill) there in the great earthquake of 1985.
14. In the San Francisco earthquake of 1989, the collapsing (= einstürzen) Bay Bridge ______ (kill) many more people if there ______ ______ (not be) an important football game on at that time.

▶ 4 *If*-Sätze

Your points: ______ /20

Mixed exercises 3

1 Ordnen Sie diese Sätze von „wenig notwendig" bis „am notwendigsten".

1. a He can do it.
   b He must do it.
   c He should do it.
   ______

2. a I am supposed to talk to him.
   b I can talk to him.
   c I had better talk to him.
   ______

3. a I had to do it.
   b I ought to have done it.
   c I was able to do it.
   ______

4. a He can see the doctor.
   b He is to see the doctor.
   c He should see the doctor.
   ______

5. a Do you have to go?
   b Had you better go?
   c Will you be able to go?

6. a She musn't call.
   b She needn't call.
   c She shouldn't call.

7. a They could have managed.
   b They ought to have managed.
   c They should have managed.

8. a You needn't have brought them.
   b You oughtn't to have brought them.
   c You weren't supposed to bring them.

▶ 5 Modale Hilfsverben

Your points: /8

2 Ordnen Sie diese Sätze von „wenig sicher" bis „am sichersten".

1. a He did it.
   b He might have done it.
   c He must have done it.

2. a He could have done it.
   b He did it.
   c He was said to have done it.

▶ 5 Modale Hilfsverben

Your points: /2

3 Übersetzen Sie die Sätze.

1. Ashley hätte vielleicht eine bessere Arbeit bekommen können.
2. Sie muss sich nächste Woche daran gewöhnen, mit einem anderen Computersystem zu arbeiten.
3. Die Firma soll angeblich nächsten Monat 10 Mitarbeiter entlassen (= dismiss) müssen.
4. Man sollte für diese Arbeit Excel benutzen können.
5. Ashley muss ihren Computer nicht selbst reparieren können.

6. Sie hätte früher aufstehen sollen, aber sie hätte kein Taxi nehmen müssen.

▶ 5 Modale Hilfsverben — Your points: /6

4 **Vervollständigen Sie den folgenden Dialog mit den entsprechenden modalen Hilfsverben.**

be able to | *get used to* | *had better* | *has to* | *have never been able to* | *have to* | *having to* | *isn't used to* | *must* | *needn't* | *ought* | *ought to have* | *said to be* | *should* | *shouldn't have* | *supposed to* | *used to* | *will be able to*

Mr Feger: Ms Gillicutt, I'm terribly sorry, but I'm afraid you'll ______ 1 work overtime (= Überstunden) this evening. These letters absolutely ______ 2 be sent out in the evening post.

Ms Gillicutt: But Mr Feger, I won't ______ 3 get my shopping done before the shops close. And I'm ______ 4 bake a cake for the office party.

Mr Feger: I really think these letters ______ 5 to be more important to you than baking a cake, Ms Gillicutt.

Ms Gillicutt: Well, Mr Feger, I think you ______ 6 ask Ms Craven to work overtime for a change. She almost never ______ 7 !

Mr Feger: Ms Gillicutt, I'm surprised you suggest that. You know that Ms Craven ______ 8 answering letters like this. It's not her field (= Bereich).

Ms Gillicutt: Well, she ______ 9 learn! And that's a warning. I'm tired of ______ 10 do the work for everyone around here.

Mr Feger: Why, Ms Gillicutt! You ______ 11 be such a pleasant person to work with.

Ms Gillicutt: I know, Mr Feger. That was my mistake. I ______ 12 kept quiet so long. But you were ______ 13 such a good person to work for. And I ______ 14 speak up for myself.

Mr Feger: Well, you really ______ [15] told me this earlier, Ms Gillicuttt. All right. You ______ [16] work late this evening. I'll ask Ms Craven if she ______ [17] stay.

Ms Gillicutt: Oh, thank you, Mr Feger. I'm sure she'll ______ [18] the work very quickly. Thank you so much!

▶ 5 Modale Hilfsverben

Your points: ______ /18

Mixed exercises 4

1 Übersetzen Sie die fehlenden Satzteile jeweils mit:

let/allow ... to + Infinitiv | have + Objekt + Partizip | have/make + Objekt + Infinitiv | be made to + Infinitiv

Wo ein (*) steht, müssen Sie **zwei** Lösungen angeben. Achten Sie auf die Wortstellung!

1. China shouldn't * ______ ______ any bigger. (seine Bevölkerung ... wachsen lassen)
2. We mustn't * ______ ______ the ozone layer. (zulassen, dass unsere Industrie ... zerstört)
3. Politicians must ______ immediately. (gezwungen werden, ... zu handeln)
4. The town council wants ______ . (einen neuen Parkplatz bauen lassen)
5. It almost ______ to see how little we do for the environment. (bringt mich ... zum Weinen)
6. Every industrial nation ought to ______ more on the environment. (gezwungen werden, ... auszugeben)

7. I'll ______ if they don't clean up the river!
(sie verklagen lassen)

8. It's fairly cheap to ______ .
(Papier wieder verwerten zu lassen)

9. The Government unfortunately won't * ______
______ wind parks offshore. (uns ... entwickeln lassen)

10. We should * ______
______ its workers about the risks.
(die Gewerkschaft veranlassen, ... zu informieren)

11. They ought to * ______ producing CFCs (= FCKW).
______
(diese Firma veranlassen, ... aufzuhören)

12. It's necessary to * ______
______ CFCs.
(jede Nation ... verbieten zu lassen)

Schreiben Sie die letzten drei Sätze neu mit get ... to.

13. We should ______
its workers about the risks.

14. They ought to ______ producing CFCs.

15. It's necessary to ______ CFCs.

▶ **6 Das Verb „lassen"** Your points: ______ /21

2 Ein dramatisches Ereignis in der amerikanischen Geschichte stellt die Schlacht am Fluss Little Big Horn in Montana dar. Dort fanden am 25. Juli 1876 General Custer und 224 Mann der 7. Kavallerie den Tod.

Setzen Sie einen Infinitiv oder ein Gerundium ein (an einigen Stellen ist dazu auch eine Präposition erforderlich). Manchmal sind zwei Lösungen möglich.

Custer decided ______ 1 (attack) the Indian village on the Little Big Horn River although he had failed (= unterlassen) ______ 2 (find out) how many warriors (= Krieger) were in it. He refused ______ 3 (wait) for assistance and dared (= wagen) ______ 4 (fight) without knowing the enemy's strength. Historians would love ______ 5 (discover) the real reason for Custer's recklessness (= Leichtsinn). In fact, anybody interested ______ 6 (read) about the battle would like ______ 7 (know) why Custer insisted ______ 8 (advance) although he had been warned ______ 9 (not do) so. It's now obvious that Custer, with not much more than 200 men, had no possibility ______ 10 (defeat) Sitting Bull and Crazy Horse. Custer was mad with ambition – he hoped ______ 11 (succeed) ______ 12 (beat) the Indians once and for all (= ein für alle Mal) and then concentrate ______ 13 (reach) his real goal: the White House. He dreamed ______ 14 (play) a great political role, but that depended ______ 15 (win) a great battle. Custer had always been used ______ 16 (act) independently, and could never resist ______ 17 (try) to get all the glory for himself. Nobody could prevent him ______ 18 (carry out) any plan he had decided on. He hated ______ 19 (lose) and had never enjoyed ______ 20 (be) second best. When one of his officers suggested ______ 21 (ask for) reinforcements (= Verstärkung), Custer chose ______ 22 (not listen) to him. He had always disliked ______ 23 (take) advice. He intended ______ 24 (encircle = einkesseln) the village with an attack from north and south at the same time, but he and his men were massacred within about twenty minutes. There were no survivors.

▶ 7 Das Gerundium und der Infinitiv

Your points: ______ /24

Mixed exercises 5

1 **Vervollständigen Sie die folgenden Sätze, indem Sie den Nebensatz in Klammern mit einem Partizip Präsens oder einem Partizip Perfekt übersetzen. Manchmal muss das Subjekt in den Hauptsatz rücken, manchmal müssen Sie ein Komma einfügen.**

1. (Da Chris sich für Elefanten interessiert) *Being interested in elephants, Chris* has booked a safari holiday.
2. (Nachdem Jim drei Stunden gewartet hatte) ______ got a photo of a rhino.
3. (Bevor der Löwe geschossen wurde) ______ killed one of the hunters.
4. The poachers (= Wilderer) were caught ______ (während sie den Fluss überquerten).
5. (Es sei denn, sie werden bald verhaftet) ______ those poachers will destroy everything.
6. (Obwohl ich mich müde fühlte) ______ decided to stay up late.
7. "It's a panda!" shouted Jim ______ (wobei er seine Kamera auf das Tier richtete).
8. (Wenn Wale nicht besser geschützt werden) ______ will disappear from the Earth forever.
9. The expedition spent a month in Nepal ______ (und hoffte dabei, dort einen Yeti zu finden).
10. "I can't find the map," she said ______ (indem sie sich an den Reiseleiter wandte).
11. (Zitternd vor Angst) ______ she watched the snake come closer and closer.

12. (Weil die Gorillas sehr scheu waren) ______ ______ kept well away from our camp.

▶ 8 Das Partizip — Your points: ____ /11

2 Übersetzen Sie den Nebensatz in Klammern mit einem Partizip Präsens und with. Und denken Sie auch an das Komma!

1. (Da viele Tiere aussterben) *With a lot of animals* *extinct,* we must protect the rest.
2. (Wenn viele Regierungen fast nichts machen) ______ ______ the World Wildlife Fund has little chance of success.
3. (Heutzutage, wo die Wälder überall abgeholzt werden) ______ ______ the climate is changing rapidly.
4. (Da Elfenbein so viel kostet) ______ ______ huge profits are being made from it.
5. (Seitdem die Nachfrage so schnell wächst) ______ ______ there's no way to stop it.

▶ 8 Das Partizip — Your points: ____ /5

3 Wo gehört der Relativsatz hin? Verkürzen Sie jeden Relativsatz durch ein Partizip Präsens oder ein Partizip Perfekt und setzen Sie ihn dann in den richtigen Satz ein.

that is threatening — *that had been made* — *who had been selling* — *which is being cut down* — *which have been opened* — ~~*that were killed*~~ — *that was running* — *who is found guilty*

1. Both the hunters *killed* yesterday will be buried tomorrow.
2. The forest ______ in Brazil at present will take hundreds of years to grow back again.
3. The greatest danger ______ the elephant's existence is the steady demand for ivory.

4. The game reserves (= Reservat) ______________ in Africa in recent years attract millions of tourists.
5. The only jeep ______________ without any problems developed some engine trouble.
6. The plans ______________ to bring food to the village couldn't be carried out.
7. The men ______________ the skins (= Fell) were all put in jail.
8. In China they have the death penalty (= Todesstrafe) for anyone ______________ ______________ of trading in panda skins.

▶ 8 Das Partizip

Your points: ______ /7

Mixed exercises 6

1 Setzen Sie who, which, that, those ein (aber nur an den Stellen, wo ein Relativpronomen tatsächlich erforderlich ist). Manchmal ist mehr als eine Lösung möglich.

Sir Arthor Conan Doyle, the author ______ [1] created Sherlock Holmes, was born in 1859. The career ______ [2] he first chose was medicine, ______ [3] he began studying at Edinburgh University in 1876. One person ______ [4] influenced him in creating Holmes was Dr Joseph Bell, ______ [5] taught at Edinburgh. Dr Bell, ______ [6] his students had great admiration for (an admiration ______ [7] Doyle never lost), could usually describe the character of any patient ______ [8] came to him in a few seconds, ______ [9] is an ability ______ [10] is also typical of Holmes. But Bell is just one of the men ______ [11] Holmes is modelled on. One other person ______ [12] character and ______ [13] habits play an important role is Doyle himself, ______ [14] has a number of similarities with the great detective – the boxing ability ______ [15] Holmes sometimes demonstrates in dangerous situations is something ______ [16] Doyle was also expert at. The other figure ______ [17] the detective has similarities with is John Doyle, Conan Doyle's grandfather, ______ [18] portrait shows a face and physique (= Körperbau) exactly like the descriptions of Holmes!

▶ 9 Relativsätze **Your points:** ______ /18

2 **Richtig oder falsch? Ersetzen Sie jedes falsch verwendete Relativpronomen durch ein richtiges; streichen Sie alle falsch gesetzten Kommas durch. (Man braucht dabei weder die Wortstellung zu ändern noch neue Kommas einzusetzen noch bestimmende Relativpronomen zu streichen.)**

1. It's the finest story, that he's ever written.

   ______

2. The man which she used to work for died recently.

   ______

3. Do you know anybody, that can translate this for us?

   ______

4. You're the one person, whose help I'm dependent on.

   ______

5. *The Man Which Was Sherlock Holmes* is the title of a biography of Sir Arthur Conan Doyle.

   ______

6. The last case that Holmes appears in was published in 1927.

   ______

▶ 9 Relativsätze **Your points:** ______ /6

3 **Vervollständigen Sie diese Sätze durch ein Adverb mit oder ohne *-ly*.**

The lovely Lady Patricia was ______ [1] (deep) worried. Her Austrian guest, Graf Sauseng, had reacted very nervously when she'd looked ______ [2] (deep) into his bloodshot (= blutunterlaufen) eyes at dinner that evening. 'Perhaps I'm not behaving ______ [3] (just) towards him,' she thought. 'After all, he's still ______ [4] (fair) tired after his week-long journey from Graz. And as for his nervousness ... well, he's ______ 5 (wide) believed to be eccentric. But last night at the ball, whenever I moved ______ 6 (close) to him, he had such fear written all over his pale face. ... I think Graf Sauseng isn't playing ______ 7 (fair) with me.' The lightning flashed. Outside, thousands of bats (= Fledermaus) flew up ______ 8 (high) into the dark night above Brompton Ralph Manorhouse. There had been a lot of thunderstorms ______ 9 (late), and the horses had been behaving in a ______ 10 (high) unusual way for days now. Patricia intended to go to bed ______ 11 (short); Graf Sauseng had ______ 12 (just) gone to his room. As usual, he had retired (= sich zurückziehen) ______ 13 (late). Suddenly, she opened her beautiful eyes ______ 14 (wide). Graf Sauseng was standing in the shadows, watching her ______ 15 (close)! Time was running ______ 16 (short) for Lady Patricia, but she remembered that Lord Finch-Hatton would be arriving ______ 17 (direct). He alone could save her ...

▶ 10 Adverbien

Your points: ______ /17

4 Vervollständigen Sie die folgenden Sätze mit einem Adverb oder Adjektiv.

The world's first vampire novel was Dracula (1897), written by Bram Stoker (1847–1912) – it's a ______ 1 (terrible) exciting book and never grows ______ 2 (monotonous) or gets ______ 3 (uninteresting) at any point. It may sound ______ 4 (strange) to say so, but its author (a government official in Dublin) was ______ 5 (unexciting) in every way. In fact, Mr Stoker looked ______ 6 (unusual) ugly and seemed ______ 7 (shy) to all those who had anything to do with him. His biographers appear to feel ______ 8 (embarrassed) that they can't find anything ______ 9 (real) amazing to tell the reader about their subject. Count Dracula, however, is quite the opposite!

▶ 10 Adverbien

Your points: ______ /9

Mixed exercises 7

1 Hier sind verschiedene Meinungen zum Thema Kernenergie (= nuclear energy).

Vervollständigen Sie die Sätze mit den Wörtern in Klammern. Das Verb müssen Sie jeweils mit einer Präposition ergänzen, um ein passendes *phrasal verb* einsetzen zu können. Achten Sie besonders auf die Wortstellung. Es genügt jeweils eine Lösung. (Die Liste der *phrasal verbs* auf S. 96–97 kann Ihnen helfen.)

1. 'There's no way we can ______ (the result/clean) of an explosion in a nuclear power plant (= Kernkraftwerk), so we should ______ (them/close) immediately.'
2. 'We shouldn't ______ (any plants/tear) until we can ______ (better ideas/work) on what to do with the used fuel rods (= Brennstäbe).'
3. 'Nuclear power is a bad idea and we ought to ______ (it/give) forever.'
4. 'We'll have no more electricity if they ______ (the reactors/switch)! And I'd like to ______ (that fact/point) to all the opponents (= Gegner) of nuclear power!'
5. If the opposition can win the next election and ______ (the government/take), they'll ______ (the plans/tear) for that recycling plant (= Wiederaufbereitungsanlage).'

▶ 11 *Phrasal verbs*

Your points: ______ /9

2 Zwei Freunde besprechen am Telefon eine bevorstehende Bergtour.

Übersetzen Sie die fehlenden Gesprächsbeiträge des Anrufers.

1. Ich werde im Sommer nach Frankreich und in die Schweiz fahren.
   ______ I'm going to go to ______ and ______.

2. Ich möchte dort mit Bernd, du kennst ihn doch, den Montblanc und das Matterhorn besteigen.

   I want to climb ______ and ______ with ______. You know him.

3. Ich werde den Wetterbericht im Fernsehen anschauen, bevor ich zur Arbeit fahre.

   I'll watch the weather report ______ before I go ______.

4. Alle Berge, die ich bis jetzt bestiegen habe, waren unter 3000 Meter.

   ______ I've climbed so far have been under ______.

5. Übrigens, hast du das Interview über den Himalaja mit dem Messner im Fernsehen gesehen?

   By the way, did you see ______ about ______ with ______ on ______?

6. Die meisten Leute haben keine Ahnung, wie schlimm die Umwelt dort bedroht ist.

   ______ have no idea how much ______ is threatened there.

7. Du hast recht! Die Umweltverschmutzung (= pollution) ist überall ein großes Problem.

   You're right! ______ is a big problem everywhere.

8. Natürlich kann dein Sohn auf unsere Bergtour mitkommen. Geht er denn noch in die Schule?

   Of course your son can come with us on our mountain tour. But does he still go ______?

9. Gut! Er spielt so gut Gitarre. Er soll doch die Gitarre mitbringen.

   Good! He plays ______ so well. He should bring ______ with him.

10. Oh, ich kann jetzt nicht mehr am Telefon weitersprechen. Mary braucht es, tschüss!

    Oh, I can't talk ______ any longer. Mary needs it. Bye!

▶ **12 Der bestimmte Artikel**

Your points: ______ /18

3 **Übersetzen Sie die unbestimmten Mengenangaben in diesem Märchen.**

The Silly Princess and the Frog Prince

Once upon a time there was a little princess who had ________ [1] (viel) time and ________ [2] (ziemlich viele) toys, but ________ [3] (sehr wenige) friends to play with. One day, she was especially bored, and asked ________ [4] (jeden) she knew to play with her, but ________ [5] (jede) person she asked had a different excuse for saying 'no'. In truth, ________ [6] (die meisten) didn't really have ________ [7] (etwas) to do. They just simply didn't want to have ________ [8] (etwas) to do with the princess, because she was ________ [9] (am meisten) thoughtless and spoiled (= verwöhnte) person they had ever met. This, of course, was why the princess had ________ [10] (weniger) fun and ________ [11] (weniger) friends than ________ [12] (die meisten) princesses.

Well, since ________ [13] (niemand) would play with the princess, she took a golden ball, one of the ________ [14] (wenige) toys that still interested her, and went into the palace garden. In ________ [15] (weniger) time than you can say 'Rumpelstiltskin', she lost her golden ball in one of the ________ [16] (vielen) ponds (= Weiher) in the garden. Our silly little princess had always had ________ [17] (wenig) appreciation for the beautiful ponds in this garden anyway, and the nasty little girl started to say ________ [18] (viele) words which you don't learn in ________ [19] (vielen) English books! Just as she was thinking there wasn't ________ [20] (viel) hope left for an interesting afternoon, a frog spoke to her from the pond. Now this was certainly ________ [21] (etwas) that she had ________ [22] (am wenigsten) expected. And ________ [23] (viel mehr) surprising was what the frog said: 'If you give me a kiss, little girl, you'll get your ball and ________ [24] (ein paar) surprises!' Now, ______ 25 (jede) sensible princess I know would have found ______ 26 (viele) reasons not to kiss a frog, but ______ 27 (wenige) of these mattered to our bored heroine. She wasted ______ 28 (wenig) time, and said: 'You haven't got ______ 29 (viel) sex appeal, you old toad (= Kröte)' – she hadn't learned ______ 30 (viel) in biology – 'but you certainly have got ______ 31 (viel) imagination.' And she kissed him! There before her was the ______ 32 (am wenigsten) handsome prince she had ever seen. And as she had ______ 33 (weniger) good sense, and even ______ 34 (weniger) good manners than ______ 35 (die meisten) other princesses, she pushed the poor prince into the pond and he became a frog again. Here he had to wait ______ 36 (mehr) years and ask ______ 37 (viel mehr) princesses until the right one came along. And our silly princess spent ______ 38 (viel mehr) days having ______ 39 (am wenigsten) fun and the ______ 40 (am wenigsten) friends of any princess I know. Which just shows you that ______ 41 (viele) princesses these days haven't read their Grimms Fairy Tales.

▶ 13 Mengenangaben

Your points: ______ /41

Teil A: Selbstdiagnose

1 Die Zeiten

2. are you doing
3. am having
4. have
5. have been trying
6. Have you driven
7. was going to
8. lasted
9. had expected
10. didn't drive
11. believe
12. has put
13. don't know
14. explains
15. saw
16. had taken
17. was driving
18. was driving
19. passed
20. wasn't
21. don't go
22. are sending
23. have been driving
24. haven't been working
25. has been
26. will be
27. am going to fly
28. leaves
29. Aren't you going to
30. will have photographed
31. am going to do
32. will be having
33. is going to give
34. will
35. will see

2 Das Passiv

2. was accused of
3. was fought
4. hadn't been given
5. is being
6. is estimated
7. were confiscated
8. can be
9. has ever been
10. had been
11. has ever been
12. were
13. will be
14. was carried out
15. was taken

3 Die indirekte Rede

2. had dreamed
3. stated
4. hadn't been
5. was
6. told me
7. had been
8. was
9. had become
10. had given
11. had been
12. could
13. had learned
14. they
15. had arrested
16. had
17. had
18. were

4 *If*-Sätze

1. will happen
2. build, will blow
3. stay, will see
4. will happen, opens
5. might learn, look
6. would, asked
7. asked, would move
8. offered, wouldn't take
9. told, would tell
10. would run, told
11. hadn't kissed, would have slept
12. wouldn't have lost, had kept
13. hadn't lost, wouldn't have found
14. wouldn't have found, hadn't kissed

5 Modale Hilfsverben

2. is said
3. ought to have
4. can
5. are supposed to
6. have
7. was able to
8. had
9. shake
10. have been
11. not been able to
12. used to
13. to walking
14. had better
15. are supposed to
16. have been
17. be able to
18. are used to
19. is
20. should
21. mustn't
22. let
23. must
24. used to be
25. Shall
26. needn't

6 Das Verb „lassen"

ohne Fehler: 1, 6, 7, 12, 14

2. allowed ... to start
3. permitted ... to search for
4. had ... marked out
5. had ... excavated
8. made ... clear away
9. allowed ... to be
10. had the door opened
11. made Carter cry
13. didn't permit ... to keep

15. had had them killed
16. made ... go out

7 Das Gerundium und der Infinitiv

3. to
4. in
5. on
6. doing
7. to do
8. to become
9. to make
10. playing
11. giving
12. offering
13. of
14. ~~to be~~ being
15. shooting
16. to admit
17. seeing
18. telling
19. to annoy
20. opening
21. from

8 Das Partizip

1. (Realizing)
2. (living)
3. (being able to)
4. (Although finding)
5. (After arriving)
6. (solved)
7. who had been arrested
8. (If given)
9. Although they didn't manage
10. (hunted)
11. (introduced)
12. (copied)
13. (hoping)
14. (Having grown)

9 Relativsätze

2. who
3. that
4. who
5. who
6. which
7. who
8. whose
9. which
10. whom
11. whose
12. which
13. who
14. which
15. which
16. which
17. whose
18. that
19. which

10 Adverbien

2. freely
3. direct
4. impossible
5. wide
6. clear
7. close
8. nearly
9. short
10. hopeless
11. dangerous
12. unbelievable
13. pretty
14. just
15. mostly

11 *Phrasal verbs*

1. point out
2. settle down
3. bring up
4. get away
5. turn up
6. built up
7. show off
8. cleaning up
9. check in
10. given back
11. closed down
12. set up
13. give in
14. carried out

12 Der bestimmte Artikel

2. the
3. –
4. The
5. –
6. –
7. the
8. –/the
9. the
10. the
11. the
12. the
13. the
14. the
15. –
16. –
17. –
18. The
19. –
20. –
21. –
22. The
23. the
24. –
25. the
26. the
27. –
28. –
29. –
30. the
31. the
32. the
33. –
34. the
35. the
36. the
37. the
38. the
39. the
40. –/the
41. the
42. the
43. the
44. the
45. the
46. the
47. the
48. the

13 Mengenangaben

2. Much
3. many
4. Each
5. some
6. each
7. more
8. nothing
9. any
10. Most
11. little

12. some
13. A few
14. any
15. some
16. every
17. more
18. fewer
19. everything
20. least
21. any
22. little
23. much
24. Some
25. any
26. many
27. less
28. most
29. many

Teil B: Grammatik und Übungen

1 Die Zeiten

Exercise 1

1. drink
2. is preparing
3. flies – gives
4. Do the Leporis make – do – are buying
5. eat
6. is cooking – likes
7. is dressing
8. does
9. do children receive – don't – receive
10. live/are living – are celebrating
11. aren't keeping
12. eat – know
13. Do they have – don't – decorate
14. are going – starts – finishes
15. Are the children looking forward to
16. start
17. is making – don't understand – is she making – break

Exercise 2

3. were baking
4. were putting
5. were practising
6. were trying
7. were standing
8. (were) ringing
9. (were) asking
10. were giving
11. happened
12. were
13. was standing
14. was counting
15. came
16. said
17. saw
18. was pointing
19. asked
20. looked
21. was counting
22. didn't notice
23. was getting
24. weren't
25. was getting
26. handed
27. interviewed
28. had

Exercise 3

1. was – was having
2. was – was driving
3. was standing – was ringing
4. was standing – was ringing
5. saw – left
6. saw – stopped
7. gave
8. saw

Santa B ist der Dieb

Exercise 4

2. haven't
3. have you been
4. came
5. Have you heard
6. have/'ve never been
7. haven't
8. have/'ve had
9. have/'ve already made
10. has been
11. have/'ve never heard
12. was
13. was
14. was
15. have forgotten
16. Have you ever been
17. have
18. went
19. was
20. haven't decided yet

Exercise 5

ohne Fehler: 1, 4, 5, 7

2. was

3. didn't enjoy
6. has been

Exercise 6

2. has been standing – for
3. have been listening – since
4. has been filling – for
5. have been selling – for
6. has been hiding – since
7. have been enjoying – since
8. have been walking – since
9. have been eating – since
10. have been holding – for

Exercise 7

1. He's/has been looking for ... since this morning.
2. How long have your neighbours been playing ...
3. How long has he been doing it/that for?
4. have been married for 50 years.
5. I've/have been reading ... since last week

Exercise 8

2. have/'ve been cleaning
3. washed
4. hid
5. have/'ve been telling
6. have (already) painted
7. have (just) celebrated
8. haven't given
9. have been telling
10. decided
11. has wanted
12. have (never) managed

Exercise 9

1. will be
2. are invited
3. will be provided

Exercise 10

Die Alternativen in Klammern sind möglich, aber weniger gebräuchlich.

2. will miss (am going to miss) – am going to continue (will continue)
3. are you going to do (will you do)
4. are going to live (will live) – am going to teach (will teach) – leave (are going to leave/will leave) – will stop (stop/is stopping)
5. Are you going to sell (Will you sell)

Exercise 11

2. is leaving
3. will live (is going to live)
4. will/'ll make
5. will bring
6. will/'ll call

Exercise 12

2. They are/'re going to pick me up
3. When do you leave/fly? – When are you leaving/flying?
4. My plane leaves/takes off – arrives/lands
5. will/'ll read a lot of books
6. I am/'m going to read

Exercise 13a

2. will have been finished
3. will have been furnished
4. will be teaching
5. will have decided
6. will be writing
7. will have opened
8. will have got
9. will be taking
10. (will be) getting

Exercise 13b

1. will be living
2. will be getting
3. will be expecting
4. will be studying
5. will be giving
6. will be attending
7. (will be) participating

8. will have completed
9. will have received
10. will have completed

Exercise 14

2. had bought
3. She had decorated
4. She hadn't borrowed
5. She had ordered
6. She had made

Exercise 15

2. was going to bring
3. was going to have
4. was going to come
5. were going to bring

Exercise 16

2. had been studying
3. had been packing
4. had been visiting
5. had been repairing

Exercise 17

2. were going to sing
3. were going to cook
4. was going to show
5. was going to be

2 Das Passiv

Exercise 1

2. has ... been informed – have been changed
3. have been dreamt
4. were spoken (would have been spoken)
5. aren't (always) required – is taught
6. have been closed – have been opened
7. will be replaced
8. have been transformed
9. are being enlarged
10. have ... been neglected – have been torn
11. are being restored – aren't being cared
12. were closed
13. have been made
14. have been modernized
15. have been balanced

Exercise 2

2. were discovered
3. have not yet been renovated
4. is being torn down – is being built (will be built)
5. is not recognized
6. are corrupted
7. It is said
8. are being carried out
9. am elected – will be made

3 Die indirekte Rede

Exercise 1

2. asked – was going to
3. insisted – had to have – their – our
4. asked – expected
5. wondered – would want
6. informed – had given
7. had no idea – they were
8. said – had been negotiating – them
9. claimed – hadn't seemed – he had talked
10. said – they would give them – they threatened – their

Exercise 2

2. they could do – our
3. we had been informed – those
4. they had received – before
5. he was – our – were
6. they would transfer – our – the next day

4 *If*-Sätze

Exercise 1

2. give
3. doesn't need
4. will/'ll sell (can sell)
5. will/'ll work

6. put
7. will/'ll give
8. give
9. comes
10. will/'ll leave
11. feel
12. will/'ll give

Exercise 2

2. would/'d never forgive
3. included
4. would/'d break
5. were/was
6. could sell
7. took
8. would ... forgive

Exercise 3

1. would only buy new cars.
2. If I only had new cars, I would have fewer repairs.
3. If I had fewer repairs, I would have more money.

Exercise 4

1. might have been sold
2. hadn't come - wouldn't have seen
3. hadn't taken - wouldn't have been
4. had been - would have been
5. had been painted - wouldn't have been sold

Exercise 5

1. hadn't been made
2. he wouldn't have taken the doll to a second-hand shop.
3. if no one had recognized and bought it.

5 Modale Hilfsverben

Exercise 1

1. can
2. couldn't/weren't able to
3. be able to
4. can't/'m not able to
5. will be able
6. wasn't able to (couldn't)
7. been able to
8. Are you able to/Can
9. be able to
10. Can (Could)
11. Can
12. been able
13. be able to
14. be able to
15. be able to

Exercise 2

1. May, A
2. Shall, F
3. allowed to, F
4. Should/Shall, A
5. Should/Shall, A
6. Can, A
7. aren't allowed to, F
8. May, F
9. May, A
10. Should/Shall, A
11. be allowed to, A
12. may (can), F
13. Shall/Should, A
14. aren't allowed to, A
15. Can, A

Exercise 3

1. have (got)/are to ... needn't/don't have to
2. mustn't
3. should/ought to
4. had better not
5. are supposed to
6. had better

Exercise 4

Necessary: I've got to do it. I must do it. I mustn't do it. I am to do it. I have to do it.
Strongly advisable: I'm supposed to do it. I had better do it.

Advisable: I ought to do it. I should to it.
Not necessary: I needn't do it. I haven't got to do it. I don't have to do it.

Exercise 5

1. We needn't/don't have to/haven't got to wear uniforms.
2. We must/have to/have got to/are to dress in a business-like way, however
3. We mustn't (aren't to) wear shorts or tight skirts.
4. You had better not come too late again. You could lose your job.
5. We ought to/should (are supposed to) interview three more applicants, but I know now who I have to hire.
6. The boss says that I'm (supposed) to work in another department next week.

Exercise 6

1. g, must/has to
2. c, may/might/could
3. h, may/might/could
4. e, must
5. j, may/might/could
6. b, may/might/could
7. a, can't
8. f, may/might/could
9. i, may/might/could
10. d, must

Exercise 7

1. These printers are said to be the best on the market.
2. They are supposed to cost less, too.
3. He's supposed to be in Hamburg.
4. Ergonomic stools are considered to be better for your back.
5. Crime is thought to be one of the biggest problems in this area.
6. Maria is said to know a lot of languages.
7. This canteen is said to have very good food.
8. Yoga is considered good for one's concentration.

Exercise 8

1. have had
2. have tried
3. must have been
4. may/might/could have gone
5. may/might/could have been moving
6. may/might/could be going
7. may/might/could be flying to Milan.
8. is supposed to be/is said to be/is thought to be an excellent programmer.
9. may/might not be driving to the conference next weekend after all.
10. is said/supposed to be getting married next week.

Exercise 9

1. used to
2. didn't use to
3. didn't use to
4. used to
5. used to
6. used to
7. didn't use to
8. used to
9. didn't use to
10. didn't use to

Exercise 10

1. He wasn't used to sitting so much.
2. He wasn't used to being on the phone so often.
3. He wasn't used to never having time off during the day.
4. He was used to hearing customers' complaints.
5. He was used to having little time for a lunch break.
6. He was used to going to work on foot (walking to work).

7. He had to get used to going to work by train.
8. He had to get used to speaking a lot of English with customers.
9. He had to get used to spending many hours a day on the computer.

6 Das Verb „lassen"

Exercise 1

2. allow everyone to obtain
3. not let big cities become
4. don't permit women to marry
5. not let its population increase

Exercise 2

Hier ist *have* in der Umgangssprache überall mit *get* austauschbar.

1. built
2. have improvements introduced - have things organized
3. have new containers designed
4. have these containers produced
5. didn't have a recycling plant constructed
6. will have the river cleaned up - have them sued

Exercise 3

2. to do
3. make the public understand - be made to realize
4. is made to melt
5. make skin cancer increase
6. aren't made to take
7. have scientists develop - not have them do
8. have every state sign - make you cry

Exercise 4

2. Get ... to close
3. Get ... to ban
4. Get ... to protest

7 Das Gerundium und der Infinitiv

Exercise 1

Im alltäglichen Gebrauch ist jede unterstrichene *-ing*-Form unten mit einem Infinitiv austauschbar.

1. <u>fishing</u> - <u>playing</u>
2. <u>being told</u> - <u>showing</u>
3. not getting - not letting
4. <u>hunting</u> - shooting
5. catching - slaughtering - attempting
6. finding
7. joining - helping
8. becoming
9. trying

Exercise 2

1. It's no use living
2. busy working
3. felt like doing
4. It was no/wasn't any fun ... sitting
5. There's no denying

Exercise 3

2. to work
3. to learn
4. to have enjoyed
5. to miss
6. not having to
7. to know
8. to find out
9. to go
10. to pass
11. to get sent
12. being killed
13. to die
14. sleeping
15. feeling
16. not to stay
17. to become
18. moving
19. to introduce

Exercise 4

1. reading
2. Don't ... to buy
3. Please remember to analyse
4. She couldn't remember visiting
5. She stopped to look around
6. Hemingway couldn't stop hating
7. He went on drinking
8. She went on to discuss

Exercise 5

2. of being able to - of not fighting - to having
3. to live - in learning - of doing
4. on writing
5. on using - (from) risking
6. (with) spending - in getting transferred
7. of reporting - (in) accepting - about/at doing
8. (in) coping with - to behaving
9. of wanting
10. on putting - in forming - on adding - of describing

8 Das Partizip

Exercise 1

2. disappearing
3. Loving
4. Not being
5. After watching ... counting/Having watched ... counted (*After having* + Partizip ist zwar auch eine übliche Struktur, grammatikalisch jedoch nicht ganz korrekt.)
6. When caught ... a lion
7. Unless stopped ... the poachers
8. If given
9. (while) trying
10. Having to
11. After being attacked/Having been attacked
12. When sold ... a lion skin

Exercise 2

2. hoping	6. using
3. making	7. being sold
4. dying	8. paying
5. freeing	9. aiming

Exercise 3

2. With the number of poachers rising/increasing
3. with so many people hunting them.
4. With (the) elephants disappearing/vanishing faster and faster/quicker and quicker
5. With so many being shot
6. With the situation having become/got so bad

Exercise 4

2. used
3. accused
4. destroying
5. occurring - happening
6. being made
7. being carried out - threatened
8. being burned
9. murdered - protected

Exercise 5

2. judging by/from
3. health permitting
4. Generally speaking
5. considering that
6. weather permitting
7. talking of
8. provided that

9 Relativsätze

Exercise 1

2. j	7. c
3. h	8. d
4. a	9. e
5. b	10. f
6. i	11. k

Exercise 2

Die Relativpronomen in Klammern können weggelassen werden.

1. whose - (that/which)
2. that/who - that/which
3. whose - whose - (that/which)
4. (that/who) - (that/which)

Exercise 3

2. cigars, which ... pipe, - scuttle, which
3. tobacco, in which
4. morphine, which
5. Watson, who ... with, - Watson, to whom ... genius,
6. companion, whose
7. case, which ... time, - rooms, whose ... opened,

Exercise 4

Die Relativpronomen in Klammern können weggelassen werden.

2. (that/which) the great detective appears in
3. whose name Holmes will always be connected with
4. who Holmes fights against

Exercise 5

2

10 Adverbien

Exercise 1

2. late	9. near
3. highly	10. wide
4. lately	11. close
5. mostly	12. pretty
6. widely	13. fair
7. fairly	14. just
8. justly	15. nearly

Exercise 2

2. appears/seems to live
3. isn't likely to stay/remain
4. keeps on trying to break
5. appears/seems to fall in love with - in fact/you see
6. are known to be
7. may/might start/begin laughing/to laugh
8. 'll be certain/sure to enjoy

Exercise 3

2. Rarely did Hollywood make
3. Seldom has there been a movie
4. Not until recently/Only recently did it become
5. Down comes a spaceship - out get some teenagers

Exercise 4

1. great - fantastically
2. seriously - Simply - crazy - unbelievable - impossible - fast - awful
3. horrible - terrible - dull - tired - unrealistic - sensibly - publicly

11 *Phrasal verbs*

Exercise 1

2. set up
3. pointed out
4. carry out - tear down
5. do away with
6. keep up with - queue up
7. dry up
8. break off - wake up

Exercise 2

2. put up with the situation
3. put it off
4. take away their natural resources/take their natural resources away - give them back
5. get along with the poor nations
6. keep it up
7. clear up the mess/clear the mess up
8. tear them all up
9. turn down requests for aid

12 Der bestimmte Artikel

Exercise 1

2. the
3. -
4. -
5. -
6. the
7. the
8. -
9. the
10. -
11. -
12. the
13. the
14. the
15. -
16. -
17. -
18. -
19. -
20. The
21. the

Exercise 2

3. the
4. -
5. -
6. the
7. -
8. -
9. the
10. The
11. -
12. the
13. the
14. the
15. the
16. the
17. -
18. the
19. -
20. the
21. the
22. -
23. the
24. -
25. the
26. the
27. the
28. -
29. the
30. -
31. -
32. -
33. the
34. the
35. the
36. the
37. -
38. the
39. the
40. the
41. the
42. the
43. -
44. -

13 Mengenangaben

Exercise 1

1. some
2. anything
3. Everything - was - an
4. anything
5. each
6. any - experience - a
7. Some
8. nobody - any - knowledge
9. a - anywhere
10. some - some (any)

Exercise 2

1. very little
2. Most - much - a lot of
3. Most of the - a few
4. quite a few - many
5. All of the - too little
6. The most
7. a few - most of the - quite a few
8. too much - too little - too few - a lot of

Exercise 3

2. fewer
3. little
4. much
5. most
6. least
7. less
8. a lot of/more - few/fewer
9. a few

Teil C: Mixed exercises

Mixed exercises 1

Exercise 1

1. has asked/has been asking
2. knew – insisted
3. lasts
4. will last
5. made
6. was sitting – noticed – discovered
7. have known
8. have measured/have been measuring
9. will/'ll check
10. will tick
11. are going to start/are starting
12. will be using/will use
13. won't be/will not be
14. are wearing
15. didn't start
16. found
17. wanted – had forgotten
18. leaves
19. are assembling
20. comes

Exercise 2

1. was chosen
2. had been considered
3. wasn't acknowledged
4. is measured
5. has been used
6. is being discussed
7. are produced
8. are being made
9. won't be known
10. were being discussed

Exercise 3

1. have been
2. feel
3. have been
4. arrived
5. has been filled
6. started
7. are
8. has been ruled
9. liked/like
10. was built
11. was
12. leaves
13. takes
14. had been
15. said
16. hadn't seen
17. arrived
18. were having
19. were running
20. (were) throwing
21. was hit
22. looked
23. was going to have
24. didn't want
25. has been described
26. (has been) photographed
27. was
28. stopped
29. are being renovated
30. be seen
31. have been
32. haven't done
33. have been sitting
34. writing
35. drawing
36. enjoying
37. is
38. are going to visit
39. will be taken
40. won't forget
41. Have you ever ridden
42. will have travelled
43. will be sitting

Mixed exercises 2

Exercise 1

1. was – was
2. was – him – had
3. he – was dying
4. expected – would do
5. he – had done – his
6. lived – ate – drank
7. his – had been
8. he – was – there – he – wasn't – there
9. happened – happened – observed – would find
10. had been made
11. could fool – could fool – couldn't fool
12. he – had found
13. was – had ... been – was
14. could – did – couldn't – taught

Exercise 2

1. didn't panic
2. would you do
3. had followed – hadn't flown
4. Be – walk
5. would pay
6. would have lost – had reached
7. were – were
8. wouldn't have hit
9. use – breaks
10. lived
11. don't build
12. will survive
13. wouldn't have been killed
14. would have killed – hadn't been

Mixed exercises 3

Exercise 1

1. a, c, b	5. c, b, a
2. b, a, c	6. b, c, a
3. c, b, a	7. a, b/c, c/b
4. a, c, b	8. a, b, c

Exercise 2

1. b, c, a	2. a, b, c

Exercise 3

1. Ashley might have been able to get a better job.
2. She has to get used to working with a different computer system next week.
3. The firm is said/is supposed to be dissmissing ten employees next month.
4. One ought to/should be able to use Excel for this work.
5. Ashley needn't/doesn't have to/hasn't got to repair her computer herself.
6. She should have gotten up earlier, but she didn't have to take a taxi.

Exercise 4

1. have to
2. must
3. be able to
4. supposed to
5. ought
6. should
7. has to
8. isn't used to
9. had better
10. having to
11. used to
12. shouldn't have
13. said to be
14. have never been able to
15. ought to have
16. needn't
17. will be able to
18. get used to

Mixed exercises 4

Exercise 1

1. let its population grow/allow its population to grow
2. let our industry destroy/allow our industry to destroy
3. be made to act
4. to have a new car park built
5. makes me cry
6. be made to spend
7. have them sued
8. have paper recycled
9. let us develop/allow us to develop

10. have/make the (trade) union inform
11. have/make his firm stop
12. have/make every nation ban
13. get the (trade) union to inform
14. get this firm to stop
15. get every nation to ban

Exercise 2

1. to attack	13. on reaching
2. to find out	14. of playing
3. to wait	15. on winning
4. to fight	16. to acting
5. to discover	17. trying
6. in reading	18. (from) carrying out
7. to know	19. losing/to lose
8. on advancing	20. being
9. not to do	21. asking for
10. of defeating	22. not to listen
11. to succeed	23. taking
12. in beating	24. to encircle/ encircling

Mixed exercises 5

Exercise 1

2. After waiting/Having waited for three hours, Jim
3. Before being shot, the lion
4. (while) crossing the river.
5. Unless arrested/If not arrested soon,
6. Although feeling tired, I
7. pointing his camera at the animal.
8. If not protected/Unless protected better, whales
9. hoping to find a yeti there.
10. turning to the tour guide.
11. Trembling/Shaking with fear
12. Being very timid, the gorillas

Exercise 2

1. becoming
2. With a lot of/many governments doing almost nothing,
3. With (the) forests being cut down everywhere,
4. With ivory costing so much,
5. With (the) demand growing/increasing/ rising so fast/quickly,

Exercise 3

2. which is being cut down
3. that is threatening
4. which have been opened
5. that was running
6. that had been made
7. who had been selling
8. who is found guilty

Mixed exercises 6

Exercise 1

Die Relativpronomen in Klammern können weggelassen werden.

1. that/who	10. that/which
2. (that/which)	11. (who/whom)
3. which	12. whose
4. that/who	13. (whose)
5. who	14. who
6. who/whom	15. (that/which)
7. (that/which)	16. (that/which)
8. that/who	17. (that/who)
9. which	18. whose

Exercise 2

1. story that ... (kein Komma!)
2. whom ...
3. anybody that ... (kein Komma!)
4. person whose ... (kein Komma!)
5. *The Man Who/That* ... (Der eigentliche Titel dieser Doyle-Biographie enthält das Pronomen *who*.)
6. Dieser Satz ist richtig.

Exercise 3

1. deeply
2. deep
3. justly
4. fairly
5. widely
6. close
7. fair
8. high
9. lately
10. highly
11. shortly
12. just
13. late
14. wide
15. closely
16. short
17. directly

Exercise 4

1. terribly
2. monotonous
3. uninteresting
4. strange
5. unexciting
6. unusually
7. shy
8. embarrassed
9. really

Mixed exercises 7

Exercise 1

1. clean up the result - close them all down
2. tear down any plants/tear any plants down - work out better ideas/work better ideas out
3. give it up
4. switch off the reactors/switch the reactors off - point out that fact/point that fact out
5. take over the government/take the government over - tear up the plants/tear the plants up

Exercise 2

1. In summer - France - Switzerland
2. Mont Blanc - the Matterhorn - Bernd
3. on TV- to work
4. All the mountains - 3,000 metres
5. the interview - the Himalayas - Messner - TV
6. Most people - the environment
7. Pollution
8. to school
9. guitar - the guitar
10. on the telephone

Exercise 3

1. a lot of
2. quite a few
3. very few
4. everyone
5. each
6. most of them
7. anything
8. anything
9. the most
10. less
11. fewer
12. most
13. no one/nobody
14. few
15. less
16. many
17. little
18. a lot of
19. many
20. much
21. something
22. least
23. much more
24. a few
25. every
26. a lot of
27. few
28. little
29. much
30. much
31. a lot of
32. least
33. less
34. fewer
35. most
36. more
37. many more
38. many more
39. least
40. fewest
41. a lot of